FACETS
OF A
DIAMOND

OTHER BOOKS BY DR. JOHN DIAMOND

FACETS
OF A
DIAMOND
Reflections of a Healer

JOHN DIAMOND, M.D.

ENHANCEMENT BOOKS
RIDGEFIELD, CT

Facets of a Diamond: Reflections of a Healer
First edition published by North Atlantic Books, Berkeley, 2002
Second edition published by Enhancement Books, Ridgefield, 2003

First Edition Copyright © John Diamond 2002
Second Edition Copyright © John Diamond 2003

Published by: Enhancement Books
               P.O. Box 152
               Ridgefield, CT 06877
               Website: www.vitalhealth.net
               E-mail: info@vitalhealth.net

Printed in the United States of America

Cover and book design/production by Jan Camp

Cover photograph by John Diamond

Publisher's Cataloging-in-Publication
(Provided by Quality Books, Inc.)

Diamond, John, 1934-
   Facets of a Diamond : reflections of a healer / John
Diamond. –2nd ed.
   p.cm.
   Includes bibliographical references and index.
   ISBN 1-890995-17-7

   1. Holistic medicine. 2. Healing. I. Title.

R733.D467 2003   610
                         QBI03-200082

1 2 3 4 5 6 7 8 9 / 07 06 05 04 03 02

To these healers who have influenced and guided me—

Louis Cholden, M.D.
Robert Fulford, D.O.
George Goodheart, D.C.
Frank Graham, M.D.
John Kerridge, M.D.
Willy May, D.D.S.
Ainslie Meares, M.D.
Hans Nieper, M.D.
Owen Potts, B.R.C.P.

With thanks to my students and friends—
Anne Allwood, Michael Garber and David Richard

And most of all to Suzie, with all my love.

TABLE OF CONTENTS

I.
FACETS
OF A
DIAMOND

I COULD HAVE WRITTEN in a more orthodox manner: "proper" lay-out, "proper" chapters. My therapy isn't orthodox, so why should my writing be? For it is part of my therapy.

I chose the present format because it is more therapeutic.

Could there be a better reason?

The meaning of the whole stems from its centre.

—Mark Musa[1]

And the meaning of my holistic healing stems from its center—me, John Diamond.

In the following pages I will reveal to you many facets of me, all to build up a picture of one holistic practitioner and thus his practice.

And I hope the more you learn of my practice—and me—the more you may learn how to help yourself, to empower yourself, to raise your Life Energy so as to heal yourself.

I am a practitioner of,
a teacher of,
a philosopher of,
holistic healing.

HOLISTIC HEALING WAS, I believe, the Medicine that was—and must come
again if we are ever to be not just kept alive, but healed, made whole.

AWARENESS AND INTENTION

*I can't emphasize enough that you must commit yourself
to your own health.*

—ROBERT FULFORD, D.O.

MY WORK IS threefold:

To make you exquisitely aware of the precise nature of your suffering—aware not just in your mind, but in your heart as well.

To actuate your intent, your will to be well, your commitment to overcoming your suffering.

And then, to step back and allow your Life Energy to go about Its work.

My work is to get It to do the work.

*The wise physician would be a watchful, but quiet spectator of
the operations of nature.*

—JEFFERSON

WHAT BINDS TOGETHER all the myriad aspects of holism is a central core philosophy. Without it, whatever one does has no real meaning.

Here is the philosophy of my particular system of healing. Not so much what I do, but why I do it, and, therefore, who I am doing it. For I am what I believe—and I believe in holistic healing, deeply.

A melody is greater than the notes
that comprise it.
It is a gestalt,
"so unified as a whole
that its properties cannot be derived
from a simple summation of its parts."[2]

Holistic therapy is such a gestalt.
To dissect out its components
is to destroy its holism.

And the sufferer is a gestalt,
a summated unified entity
greater than his elements.

And the therapist, too,
is a gestalt,
a summation greater
than the techniques
he may employ.

Therefore,
ask not what I do,
but who I am.

I WILL NOT BE FACHED!

We are not saved by what we do, only by what we are.

— ANANDA K. COOMARASWAMY

Fach: A LINE OF WORK, a department of activity *(Oxford English Dictionary)*. It is a German word, probably best translated as "pigeonhole."

When my wife says she's an opera singer, she is always immediately asked whether she is a soprano, mezzo, or alto. When she replies that she is a soprano, the next question is always whether she is a coloratura, lyric or dramatic soprano.

There is always the effort to categorize her, to pigeonhole. The interest is not in how well she sings, how lovingly, but the immediate subdivision. Not "You're a soprano—wonderful!" but "You're a soprano—what type?"

And it is much worse in Germany. There they want to know the precise, exact, minute soprano *fach:* Are you a Soubrette, a Lyric Coloratura, a Dramatic Coloratura? Or are you a Dramatic Soprano, a Lyric Soprano? Or a Spinto Soprano, a Lyric Spinto Soprano? Or even a Wagnerian Soprano?

And as the agents *fach* her, so she is permitted to sing—and no more: Musetta, but not Mimi, Constanze but not Blondchen, Lucia but not Tosca.

But she can sing them all wonderfully—her way. For, within her limits, and they are much more extensive than her designated *fach*, she is a great singer. (And part of being great is to know your limits.) And like every great singer, she brings to every role all of herself: her training, her experience, her knowledge, her enthusiasm, her heart—her whole Self.

Who are you?

I'm Susan Burghardt Diamond, a great opera singer. Don't tell me what I can sing, but what you want me to sing—and I'll tell you whether I can.

And what are you? they ask me.

I'm a holistic healer.

But what do you do? What fach can I put you into?

To which I reply: Tell me of your suffering, and I'll tell you whether you are within my limits.

Don't ask me my *fach*, and don't tell me your diagnosis—for that is your *fach*. Healing knows no *fachs*. It is all of me, and all of you.

I AM ME

I am or have been:
a doctor of medicine,
a psychiatrist,
an acupuncturist,
an applied kinesiologist.

A musician,
a composer,
a writer,
a poet,
an artist,
a photographer,
a recording engineer.

A son,
a father,
a grandfather.

A husband.

An Australian,
an American.

etc, etc, etc.

I am Me.
And All of Me
I bring to You,
All of You.

THERAPEUTIC INTENT

It is difficult to put a name on my healing work. Perhaps the best is Holistic Therapy.

It is my belief that all suffering, whatever its particular form, can best be alleviated by helping to enhance the sufferer's Life Energy, his own Healing Power.

And this may best be achieved by actuating his Creativity. This is my basic therapeutic intent.

Holistic does not mean
doing all things,
but bringing
all of yourself
to all of the sufferer,
and him bringing
all of himself
to you.

Whole to whole,
reciprocal holism.

Like playing
a perfect
duet.

II.
HOLISTIC HEALING

———❧◉❧———

JUST TO BE

I'M ALWAYS BEING ASKED to explain what exactly a Holistic Healer does.

But does he actually have to *do* anything?

All that matters is helping the sufferer to raise his Life Energy. Sometimes I think of It as being like the head of a turtle. When the environment is safe, It will emerge—and not until then.

The Holistic Healer doesn't have to do anything. Just to Be—to Be there, wholly. Wholly, and thus creating an environment of safety by his presence, not by his actions.

Then, too, the sufferer can Be Wholly—with all his Life Energy restored.

HOLISTIC OR WHOLISTIC?

WHICH IS BETTER: *holistic or wholistic?*

I much prefer *holistic* for several reasons. Firstly, it is obviously related to its root, *kailo*, from which is also derived *health* and *healer*. Therefore, one can spell it so it reminds us that healing must be holistic.

Until the fifteenth century, *whole* was spelled *hole*, the *w* being added rather as an affectation. So *holistic* is more historically accurate, and meaningful.

On the other hand, to spell it *wholistic* is to remind us that the whole of the healer must be devoted to the whole of the sufferer to help him make himself whole. So, both spellings can be of help to us.

It is interesting that the word, however spelled, is only of very recent usage. The first to appear was *holistic* in 1926, and *wholistic* was derived from it, first appearing in 1941.

The word *holistic* was coined by Jan Smuts[3] "to designate the tendency in nature to produce wholes (i.e. bodies or organisms) from the ordered grouping of unit structures."[4]

The first appearance of *holistic* in terms of the healing arts was much later—1960. There were many holistic healers—many—before then. But they didn't know that is what they were! I often wonder what they called themselves.

AN UNDERSTANDING
OF HOLISTIC THERAPY

We shall see the whole sky all diamonds.

— CHEKHOV

UNTIL I FIRST CAME to America I had never seen the northern sky. In Australia I was quite able to identify the constellations, but in America I couldn't. I searched and searched for Orion's belt, and in the end it was pointed out to me. After that I was able to find it easily.

Now, we must remember there is no Orion's belt in the sky. There is only a collection of stars that appear to us, once they are pointed out, to resemble what we imagine Orion's belt to have been. But there is no more relationship between the stars comprising the belt than there is between all the stars in the universe. The only relationship is that which we have created in our own fantasy.

A medical diagnosis is like Orion's belt. It doesn't really exist. It is just putting together a few easily observed findings that seem to have some special relationship. But when we do this, we ignore all the thousands of other findings that are really just as equally related and equally important in the whole universe of the patient.

Each patient is a universe, and a true understanding of him is an understanding of each star in that universe and of the relationship between each star and all the other stars that comprise his universe. Not just picking on a few of the stars because they make a convenient story. A true understanding of a patient is an understanding of his total universe.

This is holistic therapy. It is not twenty or so specialists each working on a patient's individual stars, but one therapist who at all times works with an understanding and appreciation of the individuality of each star and, at the same time, the myriad interrelationships of all the stars of the patient's universe. This is true holistic therapy.

Let's change our analogy. A potter is throwing a pot. While it is spinning on the wheel he is constantly feeling and examining it, using all of his aesthetic, artistic and intuitive faculties as well as his logical faculties.

Using thus his whole creative self, he works with and molds the clay to keep it as perfectly symmetrical as possible. Should one area start to become asymmetrical, he proceeds to rebalance this and to re-center this area, never working on only that area but always on the whole pot spinning on the wheel. Always working on the whole pot: his hands going up and down over the whole pot but concentrating most on the particular area that requires his immediate attention to restore the balance.

He doesn't give that particular area a special name. He doesn't feel that there is a specific problem with that part of the pot or that separate work must be done there. He just sees that in the overall dynamic structure, which is that revolving pot on the wheel, there is one area more than the others that requires his particular attention to center it. But he always works on the whole pot.

And when the whole pot has been re-centered, he then looks again at it rotating on the wheel. Now all of his brain, his intuitive brain and his logical brain, recognizes that symmetry has been restored. He proceeds to work on it again, and he keeps on working until such time as he feels that the form that he wanted has been achieved and that the pot is balanced and centered and perfect in every way.

When this point is reached, his artistic needs are satisfied, and he now feels that the pot is ready to leave him, to go out into the world on its own—balanced, centered, a thing of beauty, an aspiration to Heaven and an inspiration to Earth. By its very presence, reminding us of all that is perfect and balanced and peaceful and calm in our existence.

So it is with a sufferer. When the therapist works in a holistic fashion with him, he is all the time working with all of him, certainly concentrating a little more here where it is needed at that time—and this changes from visit to visit—but always being conscious of the whole and always being aware that the part that most requires immediate correction, the part that the sufferer most wants corrected, is but one tiny portion of the whole and will be corrected only when the whole is corrected and balanced.

And so he keeps doing this, session by session. Rebalancing and re-centering, until the sufferer and the therapist both feel that he is now ready to go out into the world on his own. He has been centered as best as possible, strengthened as far as possible against the buffets of the world. He is now ready to go out as a therapeutic communication to the world, spreading his peace, his balance and calmness and joy and love to all. The balanced, centered, integrated creature that exists inside each of us.

But remember that whenever the potter concentrates exclusively on one part of the pot, which for some reason he feels, rightly or wrongly, requires more attention, the integrity of the whole structure will be destroyed. He can shape and create symmetry and perfection only when he is always working up and down and around the whole structure. That is my understanding of holistic therapy.

Forget the medical diagnosis. It is only a name. It is only an Orion's belt in the whole firmament of the universe of the sufferer. The therapist must breach the narrow confines that most institutions want him to work within. He must think of the totality of the sufferer. To see him as anything less, to reduce his existence to a diagnosis, is an insult. To see him in his totality is to worship him as a Being.

Holistic therapy really implies the absence of using any diagnostic label. The best label is the name of the patient, because we each suffer from the disease which is ourselves. The diagnostic label for John Smith is "John Smith."

The holistic therapist must remember that the sufferer is, at this moment in time when we see him, at the end point of all the shaping forces that have influenced him in his existence. He is at this moment the sum total of his genetic endowment, of the nutritional status of his parents and of himself, of their emotional states and desires, and of his own. He is the culmination of all the shaping social forces that have acted on him and his family up until this minute.

When the holistic therapist observes the firmament of the sky that is the sufferer, he is seeing an instantaneous picture of all the end points, of all the shapings, the ebbs and flows of the universe since the beginning of time that create that picture. He knows that in the next instant, and for every instant after that, the picture will change and will continue to change with all the shaping forces of the universe.

So when he looks at a sufferer, he must remember that he is seeing him as the end product of all that has been, and realize that this will change in the future just as surely as it has changed in the past and developed into that which he sees now.

This is the only way that the holistic therapist can ever think of any sufferer. And he aspires that, with his help, the sufferer's universe may be somewhat more luminous and harmonious.

The holistic healer
sees all of himself
as one,
and all of the sufferer
as one too.
And both of them together
as one,
and that one
as part of the One.

AN INTRODUCTION
TO HOLISTIC THERAPY

THE *Oxford English Dictionary* defines *holistic medicine* as "a form of medical treatment that attempts to deal with the whole person and not merely with his or her physical condition."

It gives the following quotation: "Where traditional Western medicine identifies and attacks symptoms, holistic medicine seeks to identify the underlying conditions in the client's life that have caused the illness or allowed it to happen, and then to alleviate them."

I much prefer to use the word *therapy* rather than *treatment*, especially as I no longer practice medicine, for, as you will see later, the word *treatment* negates the concept of holism, as, to a large extent, does the very word *medicine*. I regard the term *holistic therapy* as much more satisfactory—remembering that the word *holistic* is derived from the root meaning "whole, unharmed, well." And from it is derived not only *whole* and *wholesome*, but also *heal* and *healthy*, *holy* and *hallow*.

Only holistic therapy can restore wholeness. Only holistic therapy can heal and promote health. And it can do this because it remains always "concerned with wholes rather than analysis or separation into parts" *(American Heritage Dictionary)*.

As I said before, holistic therapy really requires the absence of any diagnostic label (an essential in medicine). The best label is the name of the patient, because we each suffer from the disease that is ourselves. The diagnostic label for John Smith is "John Smith."

Now what of the therapist? What does he really do? I am John Diamond, and the only real label for what I do is "John Diamond." Even two surgeons performing the same operation give somewhat different treatments, for each is a different person. But with therapy, as distinct from treatment, the individual differences become much more important, and even more so when the therapy is holistic. For the holistic therapist brings all of himself, his totality, to the therapeutic situation.

To work with the sufferer I must examine him, get to know him, from many different aspects, trying always to amalgamate all of these facets into the total, entire unity that is him. And he must be encouraged to do the same with me. The more I know of the totality of John Smith, the more I can help him, and the more John Smith knows of the totality of John Diamond, the more he can be helped by me.

In the following pages I try to present to you some of the aspects of me, John Diamond, as a holistic therapist.

There are many holistic therapists, each a unique individual. This is a presentation of one of them.

THE DOCTOR OF OLD

FROM MY READING OF medical history, it seems to me that the doctor of old was much closer to what I call a holistic healer than to the white-coated, circumscribed, coldhearted, mechanistic, materialistic doctor of today.

He, like Hippocrates, was concerned with the patient's Life Energy, recognizing this and not his ministrations as being the major curative agent. In the main, the medicines he gave were beneficial and rarely harmful—few "side effects." (Mercury was an exception!) He cared for his patient—body, mind and spirit. And ministered to all of him as best he could, sometimes seeming more a person than a doctor.

And he knew about the soul, and ministered to it—read Sir Thomas Browne's *Religio Medici*. And of the will to be well—read Sir Thomas Sydenham.

But, most of all, read Maimonides and Paracelsus. And later Sir William Osler. They were holistic healers, as were the great majority of their colleagues, through the centuries—more, the millennia.

It is only in the twentieth century that it has changed.

There could have been, should have been a wondrous synthesis of the wisdom, humanity, and compassion of the old and the wondrous technology of the new. Instead, the old, the kindhearted, was slain by the merciless.

Have I forsaken Medicine? Never! Only that portion of it which today purports to be the whole—modern medicine. It has forsaken me, all of us.

I embrace Medicine as lovingly, as enthusiastically, as when I first started.

And I mourn over what they have done to Her.

THE RENUNCIATION OF PSYCHIATRY

I AM NO LONGER A PSYCHIATRIST. I renounce it. I renounce psychiatry because I believe cruelty is at the core of the profession. I will give just the first two examples that come to mind.

In my early days in psychiatry the head psychiatrist of a hospital took me aside, placed his arm around me paternally, and offered to teach me the first lesson of private-practice psychiatry. "John," he said, "do what I do. Put them in a private hospital for a couple of weeks and give them shock treatment. If they are not better by then, certify them to a mental hospital. That way you will have no trouble, and by then you'll have got most of the money you are going to get out of them anyway." He meant it—and that was how he practiced psychiatry.

The head of another psychiatric hospital was even crueler. At a clinical meeting a new patient was presented to him—a young girl of twenty, extremely disturbed. Her suffering was pathetic. She was obviously schizophrenic and required, most of all, loving care. But no, he proclaimed that she wasn't schizophrenic at all, merely hysteric. The treatment for this, he further proclaimed, was to "encourage her flight into health." I and others protested. But he looked at me and with a supreme pontifical gesture issued the dictum, "No, John, you are absolutely wrong. There is nothing schizophrenic about this girl. I will cure her," and again he used that phrase, "by encouraging her flight into health."

By this he meant that the staff, both junior doctors and nurses, was encouraged to do everything possible to humiliate her, to shame her, to embarrass her, to belittle her—anything and everything to abuse her, to inflict acts of minor cruelty on her, and even more, they were encouraged to think of her cruelly.

This went on, despite our protests, for two months. It finally stopped when this tortured woman jumped out of a window in the psychiatry ward and landed on the concrete courtyard some stories below. I was the first to her. Her legs were caught up under her, twisted and broken, her face was smashed and horribly distorted, blood everywhere. She looked at me with her one open eye and out of her twisted bloody mouth came,

"Maybe the doctor will believe me now." Such had been her "flight into health."

She spent many months in a surgical ward—and then was certified to a mental hospital.

I do not mean to say that all psychiatrists are cruel; I can think of many glorious exceptions, going back to Benjamin Rush. But rather that there is something inherent in the profession that tends to bring out any cruelty lurking within.

I have long wondered why this profession that should be so compassionate has, it seems to me, turned its back on humanity. It is deaf to the tormented cries, to the anguished pleas for help of the patients, the most suffering of all sufferers.

A similar profession, with similar cruelty, is that of the singing teacher—again with many wonderful exceptions. I have seen so many singers abused, both psychologically and at times physically, to the point that many of them have not only given up their careers but stopped singing altogether.

This also occurs with some teachers of instrumental music, but it is much more frequent with vocal teachers. Why? The singer stands before his teacher completely open and exposed, no instrument between them to act as a shield if necessary. He is so open, so vulnerable. He bares his breast and opens his soul to the teacher, who can reverently respond to the trust and openheartedness that the student brings to him—or hurt him. The student has placed his soul in his teacher's hands. So trusting— and so often so abused, if that is in the heart of his teacher.

And it is the same with the psychiatric patient. There is, as it were, no physical disease that can stand, if necessary, as a shield between him and his doctor. Furthermore, the ego disintegration of the psychiatric illness itself brings the sufferer's soul to the surface. There it is displayed before him, and the psychiatrist can choose to comfort it, nurture it—or not. The choice is his. So often, regardless of what superficial reason he may give—"flights into health" or whatever—the choice is really to be cruel to the helpless victim displayed before him.

Psychiatry should be at the forefront of all the therapies, pioneering, blazing a trail for all of them to follow. It, most of all, should recognize that our suffering is really in our souls. It, most of all, should be teaching love. Love rarely, if ever, appears in any index of a psychiatric text; it is not medical enough for the profession. If it proclaimed the supreme importance of love as the greatest therapy, then the profession could not tolerate cruelty within it—and furthermore would attract a different type of doctor to enter into it, those who aspire to be what Freud called ministers of the soul.

Two of my greatest mentors, the late Dr. Robert Fulford and Dr. George Goodheart, respectively an osteopath and a chiropractor, while they have deviated greatly from the mainstream of their professions, nonetheless have remained within them and have been honored by them. For, I believe, their professions are not basically cruel. My two great mentors in psychiatry were both very aware of the spiritual basis of human suffering. One stayed within the profession—and committed suicide. The other, Dr. Ainslie Meares, renounced his profession and became a teacher of meditation. I, too, renounce it to teach what I teach.

I will come back to psychiatry—gladly—when it speaks of the soul, of the spirit—of Love. When these are major topics in its learned journals.

> The sufferer's soul
> a quivering dove
> which he gives
> into my hands
> for me to help it
> fly.

That's the flight into health!

THE THERAPEUTIC ENVIRONMENT

*Driven from every other corner of the earth . . . direct their
course to this happy country as their last asylum.*

—SAMUEL ADAMS

WHEN I WORKED IN the chronic back wards of a large mental hospital, I
had more than two hundred highly disturbed and disintegrated patients
whom I was supposed to treat. But how? What could I do over and above
the usual tranquilizers? I knew all the patients by name and spoke to as
many as possible every day, reaching out as best as I knew how. But what
more could I do?

Then I realized the answer lay not in trying to treat them individu-
ally—although I tried when I could—but in treating their environment
to make it therapeutic. Improving the overall climate of their existence.

This involved many changes—all, of course, in spite of the hospital
bureaucracy. Many of the improvements were minor but critical structural changes to the wards themselves. Others were organizational.

But the biggest change was my working with the nurses, helping them
to see their major role as establishing a therapeutic climate—especially
by a change within themselves. To look around them (and, I hoped, inside
themselves) and feel what could be done to make the very walls of the
wards (as it were) part of a total healing environment. And those walls had
known many years of great suffering.

We, the nurses and I, worked to create an overall structure, a gestalt
that would itself bring healing: the organization, the physical structures,
and ourselves. (And we hoped that one day the patients would themselves be a part of the healing—an essential part.)

To quite an extent, until I was transferred to another hospital, our
plans were successful. The wards certainly became more therapeutic, to
the point where I had confidence that a newly admitted very disturbed
patient would soon settle. Not because of any drugs, but because of the
(relatively) healing climate of his new environment. And because it
offered asylum, because it was a sanctuary.[5]

There is a tendency in holistic therapy to ignore the environment of the sufferer—apart from the pollutants in it. Ignored is the overall environment, the gestalt of his existence: his physical environment and, even more so, the emotional climate—including that of his city and his country. And especially his family.

The holistic therapist needs to help the sufferer live in a therapeutic climate. And this, of course, must include the therapist's own healing environment.

Heal—whole.

A healer
tries to restore
wholeness
using his whole self.

Healer—holistic.

Heal,
from *hele*, whole.
The healer
is holistic,
because he brings
his whole self.

III.
THE HEALER
AND THE THERAPIST

—⊰◉⊱—

AM I A HEALER?

To heal is to make whole, again.

Am I a healer?
No—and yes.

No,
because only the sufferer's own Life Energy
can heal him.

Yes,
because I see my role
as helping the sufferer's Life Energy
to heal him.

My healing
is in helping him
to heal himself.

A HEALER OF SOUL SUFFERING?

Come hither, be patient. Let us converse together, because I also
tremble at myself and at all my former life.

—BLAKE

I WOULD LIKE TO CONSIDER my profession as being what Freud called "a new profession of secular ministers of the soul."

But instead of just a minister, which also has religious connotations, rather a healer. A healer of the soul suffering, a healer of the spirit. Not a spiritual healer, for I don't think of myself as healing by spirit, but instead helping a sufferer overcome his pain by encouraging the workings of the Healing Power of his own Spirit, which I refer to as his Life Energy.

So not a spiritual healer, but a healer of the spirit. I cannot try to be anything else. For all of my life I have wanted to heal. And increasingly through the years of clinical experience, I have come to realize that all distress, all disease, is really of the soul, that all suffering is basically a spiritual problem. So inevitably I come to the realization that I am a healer of the spirit. Or at least this is my aspiration.

Although I may use many modalities in my practice, only three are basic: my hands, my voice, and my intention. I try to keep this intention when I am working personally, or writing, as I am doing now—not primarily to give knowledge, but really to ease suffering. So I hope.

Often when trying to heal, I feel heat, like a flame, radiating from the center of my chest. The same as I feel whenever I read Blake. Theophan the Recluse, the Eastern Orthodox religious teacher, wrote that this sensation was an early stage of the opening of the heart. And, he went on, it would pass as one became more deeply committed. Therefore, I don't know whether when I don't have this feeling it means my intention is stronger or weaker. But I do know there are times when it is there, when my intention is to help heal a sufferer's troubled spirit.

But before I can try to help him heal himself, help him invoke his spirit, he must ask himself, at his deepest level, does he really want to be healed? And of what? The clearer he is of the exact nature of his suffering, the precise point of his pain, the easier it will be for him to be healed. For my role is to help him identify this pain and then to encourage him to overcome it by invocation of his Spirit.

A major part of my work is to help him go into himself, deeply and honestly, to find the precise fulcrum of his pain. Once we do, it is so easy to tip the balance for life and love.

HEALER AND THERAPIST

I PREFER THE WORD *healer* to *therapist*, because it sounds less medical. For a doctor of medicine to call himself a healer implies a renunciation of the medical model, and this I heartily volunteer.

On the other hand, *healer* runs the risk of becoming *treater*. As we have seen, the word *healer* comes from *whole*. A healer can see himself as being the restorer of health, of wholeness. If so, then he is as grandiose as a treater, placing himself above, even ignoring, the Healer within, the sufferer's Life Energy.

But if the healer acknowledges and reverences the sufferer's deep drive for Wholeness and desires to assist It, then he is a True Healer. And a True Healer is a True Holistic Therapist—all of his Self at the service of all the Powers within the sufferer yearning to be expressed.

A therapist does not *prescribe*—"to order the use of a medicine or treatment" *(American Heritage Dictionary)*. This word also means, relatedly, "to lay down a rule; to dictate" *(Oxford English Dictionary)*—the grandiosity of the treater.

A True Therapist does not order or dictate, for he is a servant of the sufferer's Life Energy. He recommends, suggests, and encourages—as humbly as he can.

A True Therapist, a True Healer, does not diagnose, treat, or prescribe in any medical sense. For he is concerned not with disease but, much more importantly, with Life Energy.

He is a minister, tending to the needs of the impaired Healing Powers of the sufferer.

Thus he is, I believe, a member of Freud's "new profession of ministers of the soul."

THE THERAPIST AS A HUMAN BEING

> The cure starts
> when the therapist
> is seen as a person.

THE WOMAN IS CRYING and raging—hurling invectives at her ex-husband. But he is not there to be afflicted by them—I am. And I feel them—and they hurt. For we all suffer from another's negativity, even if it is not intended for us.

With some difficulty, I manage to get her to stop her barrage momentarily. I point out to her that she is hurting me with her hatred.

Why dump this on me?—That's what you're paid for.

No, I protest. I may be a therapist, but I'm also a human being. I, too, feel pain. Suddenly she softens and apologizes and now her hatred is gone.

A major task of the therapist is to get the sufferer to move outside herself, to empathize with others—even her ex-husband. And this reaching out must include the therapist.

It's a wonderful moment for the therapist when he realizes that, for the first time, the sufferer is seeing him not as an object but as a fellow human being.

HEALING AS AN *ENDUM*

Endum IS A LATIN WORD-ENDING meaning "requiring to be done, worthy of being done." Hence, *liber legendus est*, the book is worth reading.

Consider *agenda*—from the Latin *agere*, "to act," plus *enda*, the plural of *endum*. Thus an *agenda* is a list of actions requiring to be done.

This is how I see the healing of suffering. Not as a must—he must get better; I must get him better. For who am I to command the Universe? Who am I to dictate what is best? Then I have abandoned healing and become but a treater.

I try to heal because his suffering invokes an *endum*—the healing is worth doing, it requires being done.

I do it because it is there to be done, and I have been given some power to do it. My mind, and I hope my heart, is not on the prescribed result, the ending, but on the doing, the *endum*.

SETTING AN EXAMPLE

A MIDDLE-AGED COUPLE is going through a bitter divorce. She is filled with hatred, especially indulging in scathing public attacks on his sexual inadequacies. And he has become a "simpering, whimpering child again" (with apologies to Larry Hart), bursting into public bouts of self-pitying tears, clinging desperately to her. Bereft of all power, unable to work, unable to get on with life, he is impotent, castrated.

The result of their actions is that their son, for the first time in his life, is having sexual difficulties. He has become frightened of his loving wife, as if she were as castrating as his mother. He, like his father, has become impotent.

The cause of his problem is obvious: his parents are acting entirely selfishly, doing whatever they wish—her outbursts of hate, his of childish tears—without any thought of their effects on him. Self-indulgent.

They have forgotten that one of the most important functions of parents is to set an example. And to continue to set it throughout their lives, even when their children are grown, for a parent's teaching concludes only at death. (In fact, their last teaching should be their greatest: how to prepare for death, how to accept it.)

And every teacher must set the best example for his students. The therapist must demonstrate by example how to most lovingly, most gratefully, deal with all the vicissitudes of life.

Teaching by example should be the therapist's finest teaching.

THE ZAM-BUK MAN

AT MY SCHOOL FOOTBALL matches there was always a first-aid attendant seated on a little folding stool on the sideline at midfield. He was called the Zam-Buk man because, whatever the injury, he would freely apply that strong-smelling proprietary liniment.

The point I wish to make about him, and me, and all healers is that he was allowed to run out onto the field to render assistance only when summoned by the referee. So until the referee blew his whistle, the Zam-Buk man could only sit and wait. And oftentimes, he would see an injured player writhing on the ground but could do nothing to help until summoned by the whistle.

And all healers are in a similar situation. Until we are summoned, we must sit on the sideline—and wait.

Every day I see people in suffering—relatives, friends, and strangers on the street, on the subway. My heart opens to them, but I must do—can do—nothing until they ask, until they blow the whistle for me. All I can do is open my heart—but not take them in.

It is so much easier with a beggar on the street. He is imploring help. But the others do not ask. And I must learn to wait.

To go up to them and impose myself is not meant to be my Way, nor theirs. We are not to meet.

Paracelsus[6] taught that illness is a purgatory imposed by God to cleanse the soul of the patient. And when it is cleansed, He will refer him to the appropriate doctor to be cured.

I must wait for the *Right* referrals.

Harry Edwards, the great spiritual healer, likewise wrote that the healer must never intercede to help until the sufferer requests it, or, if unconscious, a close relative.

Until then, we can only observe the play from the sideline, listening for the whistle—and always ready with the Zam-Buk.

THE THERAPIST, NOT THE THERAPY

WHAT'S WRONG WITH MUSIC therapy, psychotherapy—and every other therapy? The main problem is that they do not really exist.

Many individuals, trained or untrained, profess to practice music therapy. But it will truly be therapy only when the practitioner is therapeutic. And then he is not a music therapist but a therapist who uses music as his chosen modality by which to express his therapeutic zeal.

Without the zeal, the therapy will never be therapeutic—and even without the modality, the true therapist will still be therapeutic.

Treatment depends on the modality, but therapy only on the therapist—on the strength and purity of his therapeutic intent, on his wholehearted and passionate commitment to alleviate suffering.

SPEAKING FROM THE HEART

Your blood drove you, not to form, not to speak, but to reveal.
—RILKE TO IBSEN

WHEN THEY WERE TRYING to teach us psychotherapeutic technique, we were instructed to plan very carefully what we would say to the patient, to weigh our words very precisely. And later we would have to justify them—"Why did you say that?"

Over the years, I have come to realize the utter sterility of such a "system." All from the brain, not from the heart.

It's not what you say that matters, not the words. Only the intent.

THE DOCTOR AS POET

Earth in the harmony of her three kingdoms offers man a living fascinating and enchanting spectacle . . . with which he feels himself at one.

*—*Rousseau[7]

Body, mind, and spirit.

I started with the mind, rejecting the body, and being unaware of the spirit.

Over the years, I have become increasingly drawn to the two extremes, realizing that the mind is but an arch resting on two mighty pillars—body and soul.

Whitman sang:

I am the poet of the body,
And I am the poet of the soul.

I, too, sing the praises of the body and the soul. And I, too, write poetry, although I am not a poet.

Emerson described the poet as he "who reattaches things [I'd say people] to nature and the Whole."

Perhaps in this sense I am a poet. And, too, my therapeutic aspiration is like Keats' for poetry:

the great end
Of poetry, that it should be a friend
To soothe the cares, and lift the thoughts, of man.

Would that I was a real Poet. For, as Emerson proclaimed, "He is the true and only doctor."

There can be no poetry without the Spirit.

*—*Peter Russell, *poet*

AVOCATION, VOCATION OR *VOCATION*

Heaven is his vocation, and therefore he counts earthly
employments merely avocations.

—THOMAS FULLER

Vocation IS FROM THE LATIN *vocare*, "to call." The usual definition is a particular business or profession. It is a calling.

But there is also a higher definition: a calling by a Higher Authority to a person to carry out a special function of a spiritual nature. This I capitalize as Vocation, and Calling. Thus I would capitalize vocation in the above quotation, and in this from Ephesians: *walk worthy of the vocation wherewith you are called.*

So we have vocation and Vocation, a calling and a Calling.

I have found that only those who regard their profession as being a spiritual calling will see it as a Vocation. For example, the pianist who states that his profession is to give concerts will have only a vocation. But the one who believes that his playing is to heal suffering will believe he has a Vocation.

Only those who have dedicated themselves to healing will believe in their hearts that they have a Vocation. In a sense, they believe they have been Called to it.

So healing is a Vocation, treating merely a vocation.

I believe that the Higher Authority that Calls to the Vocation is the Highest Self. To It the healer responds, but the treater only to the lower self.

And what of *avocation*—literally, a calling away from the Vocation? It is at best but a minor occupation. So often the treater is called away— from vocation to avocation.

Every practitioner has the choice—avocation, vocation, or Vocation. It is not what he does as such that determines which one he practices, but whether he is responding to the Call of the God Within, the Spirit of Compassion.

Robert Frost wrote:

> *My object in living is to unite*
> *My avocation and my vocation*

I believe it should be more—to make all a Vocation.

Hector Berlioz wrote of the moment when he heard his calling:

[I] vowed as I left the Opera that ... I would be a musician. I actually wrote off then and there to my father, acquainting him with the imperious and irresistible nature of my vocation.

A FRAMER OF A DECLARATION

Independence is my happiness.

—PAINE

*We hold these truths to be sacred and undeniable; that all men
are created equal and independent, that from that equal creation
they derive rights inherent and inalienable; that among these are
life, liberty, and the pursuit of happiness.*

—JEFFERSON[8]

I ASK THE SUFFERER to examine his existence, honestly:

Is there Life? Is there Liberty? Is there Happiness?

My role is to help him declare his Independence.

Health is based on happiness.

—ROBERT PAITCH, M.D.,
The Gesundheit Institute

ALONG THE WAY

Half way along the road we have to go,
I found myself obscured in a great forest,
Bewildered, and I knew I had lost the way.

—DANTE[9]

AT TIMES, I AM a redirecting guiding hand.

Better still would be to help the sufferer find his Way.

THERAPY OR HEALING?

You may wonder why sometimes I speak of therapy and other times of healing. Let me explain the difference.

I use *therapy* when I am referring to the role of assisting, attending to, the sufferer's Life Energy. Particularly in contrast to the treater's role. Whereas I use *healing* when I wish to stress the heart aspects.

Therapy is a little cool, more intellectual-cerebral. It is concerned with the concept of Life Energy. It is talk of the Spirit.

But healing is hot. It is Spirit in action.

Anything can be
treatment or therapy.
It's not the modality,
but the attitude.

IV.
THE TRUE
THERAPIST

———◄❋►———

TREATMENT OR THERAPY?

To call your work
therapy,
it must enhance
the Life Energy.

THERE IS A MOST IMPORTANT difference between treatment and therapy.

Treat comes from the Latin *tractare*, whose meanings include "to handle, to manage," for example, to treat a subject poetically, or to treat one's guests with courtesy. The central meaning is "to act in a specified way with regard to someone."

And of course it means to give medical aid. For example, the treatment of appendicitis is to act in the specific way of performing an appendectomy. Giving something or doing something for a specified condition in a specified way. Handling the case as specified. Treatment can only ever be through the application of the medical model: find specifically what is wrong and then act on it in the prescribed way. Handling the case, managing it, by the application of an external influence, a prescription in one form or another.

In contradistinction to this, *therapy* comes from a Greek word meaning "inclined to serve, to attend on, to be obedient to." Rather than being the manager, as is the treater, the therapist is the servant, the attendant. He does not impose his power, but rather acts as a servant for the healing power that is within the sufferer. He places himself at the service of what Hippocrates called the *vis medicatrix naturae*, the Healing Power of Nature, which we all possess.

So chemotherapy is a complete misnomer, it really is chemotreatment. And so is nearly all of orthodox medicine. And psychiatry too, which is primarily dedicated to imposing power of one form or another on the patient so as to control or in some other way modify his disquieting behavior. There was one psychiatrist, who tragically died young, who instead proposed therapy, true therapy. This was Louis Cholden[10]:

"There is a vital force within each patient that desires fulfillment, maturation and development . . . to the maximum utilization of his potential. . . .

"The therapist must constantly keep in mind—*medicus curat, natura sanat*, the doctor looks after, nature heals—that he is not curing a disease. Rather he is creating an environment of safety, trust in people and faith in living, which allows the natural forces of health within his patient to flourish. . . .

"There can only be . . . the humility of being an accessory in the service of nature's healing forces."

This is true therapy, the practitioner dedicating himself to the service of "the natural forces of health within his patient."

True therapy raises the Life Energy, allowing the Healing Power within to bring about a cure. Whereas treatment can only ever be the amelioration of symptoms.

Long before its first manifestation, every illness lurks deep within as a loss of Life Energy, as a turning down of what I call the inner flame, as a loss of the will to be well. If this is not corrected, the specific illness, as dictated by the patient's specific diathesis, will eventually reach clinical proportions. And now if treatment is imposed, there can only ever be a reduction of symptoms, never a true cure, because treatment as such does not actuate the Life Energy. In fact, it all too frequently further diminishes it, potentially predisposing the patient to greater suffering.

Today there are so many procedures called therapies of one kind or another. But how many of them are really therapeutic? And how many of them are really treatment, albeit by less chemical or mechanical means?

I have known some medical doctors, even some surgeons, who really were therapists, like Louis Cholden, not just treaters. And I have known many so-called therapists who are really only treaters. I believe that most of them entered their chosen profession to become a therapist, but a specific trauma occurred that caused them to lose their therapeutic zeal.

She leaves
her doctor's office
as dispirited
as when she entered,
for all she received
was a piece of paper.

The modality itself is of little importance: so much depends on the individual practitioner. Does he have therapeutic aspiration? Does he have the fervent desire to help the patient? And to do it not by what he does, but what he allows and encourages the patient's own healing Life Energy, his own Healing Powers to accomplish? Can he humbly place himself at the service of the patient's Healing Power within?

The crucial test is not whether the patient gets "better" but, far more importantly, has his Life Energy been significantly enhanced? Has he been helped to embrace Life? Has he been helped to love?

The bigger the building,
the heavier the overheads.
The heavier the overheads,
the less the desire
to heal.

There comes a time
when their weight
collapses
the bridge of healing.
Only the jagged edges
remain
—as treatment.

A treater goes by
what he measures,
a healer by what
he feels.

With increasing experience,
the treater jams
ever more findings
under the same rubric.

Whereas the therapist
ever expands his rubric.

With every new day
he changes and grows,
and thus his therapy, too.

I look at my hands—
So ordinary.
With these
I try to heal!

How would
I like them to be?

Elizabeth Browning
comes into my mind:

Love came by, and having known her
In a dream, of fabled lands,
Gently stooped, and laid upon her
Mystic chrism of holy hands.

If only!

THE TRANQUILIZER NON-TRIAL

I ONCE SET UP A THERAPEUTIC trial of a new tranquilizer in the locked ward of a mental hospital where the most disturbed and dangerous patients were incarcerated.

I completely reexamined the patients, many of whom had been there for many years. And then twice a week I interviewed them again to assess any change.

At the end of the three-month trial period, I turned to the head nurse who had been supervising throughout and excitedly exclaimed that the drug had worked! The patients were obviously greatly improved!

"Yes," he readily acknowledged, smiling sagely. And then he added, "But I never gave them any of the medication." I was dumbfounded. "Then why are they so much better?"

"Doctor, they've been here for years. And no doctor before you ever gave them any attention. You yourself made the change."

Yes, I suppose I did. I—and that wise nurse who wanted to prove to me that I could. Not I—we.

And, years later, I eventually came to realize that what "we" did was to rekindle their Life Energy. It was really "they" who did it.

FORMULA OR PHILOSOPHY?

A TREATER AND A HEALER may both make the same recommendations, but there will be a fundamental difference.

The treater is acting from formula, the healer from his philosophy.

The treater may protest that he, too, has a philosophy. But it will be based only on the overcoming of disease, not the promotion of Health.

His philosophy is only from the brain, not the heart.

Even if the doctor
proclaims himself a teacher,
like all other teachers,
he will still be
either a teacher or a therapist.

The teacher-treater
imposes his own self
on the student,
but the teacher-therapist
recognizes and reveres
the unique Creativity
which is his student,
and helps him
to realize his Self.

Many treaters
and healers
have worked on
my body.
The difference is
the healer
works on me
through my body.

RENÉ DUBOS WRITES: "To ward off disease or recover health, men as a rule find it easier to depend on healers than to attempt the more difficult task of living wisely."[11]

But by "healer" he really means treater. The true healer is a teacher whose "most important function . . . is to discover and teach the natural laws which will ensure to man a healthy mind in a healthy body."

For the true healer, "health is the natural order of things, a positive attribute to which men are entitled if they govern their lives wisely."[12]

NOT TO DIAGNOSE AND NOT TO TREAT

THE TRUE THERAPIST, the Healer, never diagnoses any disease. He is not interested in this *per se,* but in the diminution and disturbance of the Life Energy, the Spiritual malaise that is the basic cause of all suffering.

Nor, therefore, does he prescribe treatment for any disease. For apart from not being concerned with the disease as such, he is not a treater but a therapist.

And for this reason any recommendations to the sufferer are directed toward enhancing the sufferer's own Life Energy, for only then can there ever be Healing.

THE SPIRIT OF ROMANCE

The True Therapist is a Romantic.
He lives in—he loves to live in—the world of Feelings.

He may well know of bones, muscles and biochemistry,
but he feels at home among Feelings.
Emotions—all of them, including the negatives.

Sometimes he feels as if he is swimming in a flood tide of Feelings,
sometimes upstream, other times down.

But always he loves the flow of Feelings—
he plays in it, sports in it, revels in it.

He loves Feelings!

And he loves to wear his own on his sleeve, proudly.

"The thirst for the infinite . . . animates the lines of the Romantic,"
wrote Mario Praz.

AND, I HOPE, their lives, too.

A Note For You

A TOUGH MIND AND A TENDER HEART

One of Martin Luther King, Jr.'s sermons is entitled "A Tough Mind and a Tender Heart."

A tough mind he said was "characterized by incisive thinking, realistic appraisal, and decisive judgment. The tough mind is sharp and penetrating, breaking through the crust of legends and myths and sifting the true from the false. The tough-minded individual is astute and discerning. He has a strong, austere quality that makes for firmness of purpose and solidness of commitment."[13]

But Dr. King went on to teach that with the tough mind there must also be a tender heart—the tenderness of the dove.

A tough mind and a tender heart. A good depiction of the True Therapist.

THERAPY
AND THE AESTHETIC EXPERIENCE

Great art is made to call forth an ecstasy.

—Ezra Pound

The essence of a High aesthetic experience is to see, to feel, to know all around you the Beauty of Existence; to come to the sudden overwhelming enlightenment that you are living in the Land of Belovedness.

Disease is the absence of this aesthetic experience, and it arises from a diminished aesthetic attitude, a greatly reduced desire to experience the Beautiful.

The True Therapist is a teacher of Art appreciation—opening the student's eyes and heart to the Giottos and Turners everywhere!

The sensation of beauty is not sensual on the one hand,
nor is it intellectual on the other; but is dependent
on a pure, right, and open state of the heart.

—Ruskin

TO ACTIVATE OR TO ACTUATE?

THE *Oxford English Dictionary* gives this quotation for *activate:* "Snow and Ice . . . their cold activated by nitre or salt, will turn water into ice." The nitre or salt, as it were, puts the energy into the snow and ice. And for *actuate:* "A vibrating diaphragm could be actuated by the human voice."

To activate is to put energy into, whereas to actuate is to bring into motion the energy already present in latent form. We change only what is already there. That is to say, with actuation we just transmute the nature of the energy from potential to kinetic. We merely cause the stored-up energy to be released. You need only actuate a device or an instrument that is primed, programmed, ready to go. You are required only to press its button.

Musical instruments require only actuation, and the better they are, the more enthusiastically they respond.

To get a musical sound from a block of wood you have to activate it, but from a drummer's woodblock you need only to actuate. The maker has already transformed it from being just a block of wood; he has already activated it. All we do is release the energy he has put in. And the better the maker, the more activation, the more potential for actuation, he has imparted to it. With the woodblock, I don't, as it were, make the sound; I only make it audible.

The treater, if he ever does think about it, which is unlikely, believes it is his Life Energy that is activating the patient.

The false therapist is somewhat better: he believes that he is activating the sufferer's own Life Energy. But activating—as if none was there before his intervention.

The True Therapist, on the other hand, believes that all he does is attempt to actuate the Life Energy imprisoned within the sufferer. He is only a releaser.

TO ACTUATE THE SUFFERER INTO SONG

Song is existence.

—RILKE

THE MUSICIAN CONTEMPLATES his instrument. How to actuate it?

The maker has already activated it, transmuting it from just a piece of wood. Long ago, at its creation.

Now, how to actuate it? How to release its inherent music?

Likewise, I contemplate the sufferer.

He, too, was activated at his creation. So I know the Life Energy is in there—but dormant, silent.

How to actuate It into a life of Song?

Even as a mother watches over and protects her child, her only child, so with a boundless mind should one cherish all living beings, radiating friendliness over the entire world, above, below, and all around without limit. So let him cultivate a boundless good will towards the entire world, uncramped, free from ill-will or enmity.

Standing or walking, sitting or lying down, during all his waking hours, let him establish this mindfulness of good will, which men call the highest state!

—METTA SUTRA[14]

IF ONLY I WERE as this. Then—at last—a True Healer.

THE AURA

That volatile essence of the soul, that aethereal aura.

—BERKELEY

Aura COMES FROM the Greek *aura*, "breath" or "vapor." And one of its meanings is a gentle wind, a zephyr. Hence, a breath, an emanation, a radiation.

"A supposed subtle emanation from and enveloping living persons . . . consisting of the essence of the individual" *(Oxford English Dictionary)*.

The aura is a manifestation of the Life Energy. Hence, a sufferer's aura is always small; he is contracted into his pain.

But when his Life Energy is raised, It so radiates that to become aware of It is epiphanic.

Just sometimes after working with a sufferer I sense that this occurs.

Just sometimes
—so far.

MY WIFE TELLS ME that when she is performing opera she so expands as to fill the opera house, taking all the audience into herself. She reaches out to bring them into her.

And, of course, her singing is so beautiful and so loving that the audience wants to enter into her open aura.

This may well be the best description of Healing. The healer opens his heart, his love pouring out from him to enfold the sufferer, to bring him into his expanded aura. And the sufferer, feeling this love, opens his heart to enter the healer's.

The fusion of their auras, their Spirits as One. All this is but an analogy for mother and child—for there is the truest Healing.

THE FUSION PROBLEM

Fusion: when two egos merge into Spirit.

FUSION—THE UNION or blending, the amalgamation, of different entities as if by melting, so as to form one whole—comes from the Latin *fundere*, "to melt."

True love is when the two hearts melt together so as to create a new being, their Love.

This, unfortunately, is rare. Most marriages suffer from a fusion problem—a reticence, a reluctance, a fear of fusing together to create this new higher Creature. And of all acts of Creativity, none is Higher than this, no work of Art greater.

And the fusion, the melting together, comes from heat, high heat—their two inner flames, their hearts on fire.

True Holistic Therapy must have such a fusion. But it is this that the would-be Therapist fears; in fact it provokes anger, for the fusion problem relates to the heart meridian,[15] specifically Heart 5.

I have many times seen therapists work superficially on the sufferer's body without any particular problem, but as soon as they start to really <u>feel</u> the sufferer, to go into him, to do real Therapy, instead of being loving, they develop (unconscious) anger.

It is this fusion problem, probably more than any other, that prevents the therapist from becoming a True Therapist. And this, of course, greatly limits the success of his therapy.

Furthermore, it is only when he is a True Therapist that he can help the sufferer overcome his own fear of fusion so that there may be True Therapy.

And this fear, like all others, is only a fantasy—only an imagined mist. And a mist soon evaporates in the heat.

True Holistic Therapy is the union of the hearts of the therapist and the sufferer, fused by their inner flames, so as to create from them both a new Therapeutic Entity, greater than either of them.

THE SUFFERER SEEKING ASYLUM

"IF THE THERAPIST MAKES some moment of life hold enough safety . . . the integrative factor can operate." So wrote Dr. Louis Cholden.[16]

Asylum is the protection offered by a sanctuary, from the Greek *asulon*, "sanctuary." A sanctuary is a place of refuge, of safety—from the Latin *sanctus*, "sacred."

So the True Therapist needs to provide a sanctuary for the sufferer, to grant him asylum, a place of peace, where he may at last heal himself.

For this reason I work not in a cold commercial office but in my home, trying as best I can to make it a sanctuary. Hoping that one day they may say of me:

> *Beneath his Roof They found asylum oft.*
>
> —BYRON

V.
THE SUFFERER

THE WILL TO BE WELL

*To burn always with this hard, gemlike flame, to maintain this
ecstasy, is success in life.*

— WALTER PATER

I HAVE A GREAT ADMIRATION for Freud, but was his practice therapeutic?
Were his patients truly healed?

The start of all illness is the loss of the inherent will to be well. In
fact, I believe that the illness itself is this loss of the will to be well, just differently manifested depending on various lesser etiological factors.

Freud's will to be well was greatly diminished some years before his
oral cancer was diagnosed. It was this diminution in Life Energy which
enabled the other potential causes to have their effect—especially his
heavy cigar smoking. He himself frequently acknowledged that the cigars
were the cause of his cancer. And time after time he was admonished
and exhorted by his friends and medical attendants to give it up. But,
except for very short periods, he persisted until his death.

His illness was a particularly miserable one with great suffering. A
part of his jaw had been cut away in an unsuccessful attempt to eradicate the cancer, and an oral prosthesis was fitted which had to be constantly readjusted. During his last years in Vienna his physician would

attend him daily in a little room next to Freud's consulting room, where bone and tissue would be painfully cut away to readjust the prosthesis. His life became increasingly one of great pain and suffering, and yet he continued to smoke—knowing it was destroying his life, knowing it would kill him.

This is an example, unfortunately not an atypical one, of the effects of the loss of the will to be well, of a diminution of Life Energy. Even if the surgery had been successful and the cancer completely eradicated, Freud would still have been basically ill, for surgery does nothing to actuate the spirit, what Freud himself described as Eros, the drive for life.

His basic illness, his loss of the will to be well, would have affected his whole family, for some of it is always passed on. This is why every serious illness is a family problem and must always be addressed as such.

And what of his patients? He would have transmitted this negativity, this turning away from life, to all of them. Yet they themselves would have come to him with this as their own underlying problem, and it would have been this more than anything else that he should have undertaken to help them overcome. But this he would have been unable to do for he himself had the same illness—and in fact he probably made their own deeper suffering worse.

Furthermore, this basic illness is increasingly present in his writings. And so we find that, brilliant as they are, even when we read them today more than half a century after his death, they (temporarily) diminish our own will to be well.

In my very first weeks as a doctor some forty-five years ago I was involved in the treatment of two young men in adjoining hospital beds, both paraplegic; the same diagnosis. They both developed the same infection, and they were both given the same antibiotic. Within a week or so one had recovered but the other had died. "Why?" I asked the senior doctor.

"Well," he replied, "some have got it and some haven't."

He didn't say any more about the "It," but I realized then that this is what really mattered, not the antibiotics, not all the other treatments, valuable as they may be. Basically, I had to learn about the "It" and how to encourage it. This I called Life Energy, and it has been, increasingly, the focus of my research and therapeutic endeavors ever since.

It was obvious that this was the essential difference between those two young men. The one who recovered was always bright and cheerful, genuinely so—not pretending. When I walked in the ward, he would be glad to see me and would give me a friendly welcome, as he gave everybody else. He continued his relationship with his girlfriend; in fact soon afterward they became engaged. He pursued his correspondence courses intensely, he did his exercises with dedication, and, perhaps most of all, he was solicitous and caring for his fellow patients. In spite of the terrible trauma he had suffered, he had "It," he had high Life Energy, he had the will to be well.

And this is exactly what the other poor man lacked. He was always a misery, never smiling, never friendly, always complaining, wouldn't do his correspondence courses, wouldn't do his exercises. He broke off with his girlfriend and increasingly turned away from his fellow patients. No "It." So with the same stress, the same infection, he succumbed whereas the other survived.

Soon after this profound learning experience I saw a woman who was deeply depressed because of her guilt over an extramarital affair. While in the hospital she developed appendicitis. What better place to get it? She would have been assured of recovery. She had a routine appendectomy, the surgery went well. And yet a few days later she was dead from pneumonia. In spite of the antibiotics and in spite of every effort of the nurses to get her to cough up the infection, which she refused to do.

Yes, I realized the "It" was what really mattered. Without the "It" there may be treatment of the symptoms, of the particular illness even, but not of the deep illness, the one basic illness which is common to every serious disease, the illness in the soul—the loss of the will to be well.

Only when there is great enthusiasm for life, only when the Life Energy is high, can the Healing Power within bring about the true cure. Life Energy, the drive for life and for love, is our greatest gift. It is this that must be actuated and enhanced, for only then can true healing ever occur.

Let me tell you about the first four sufferers that come to mind out of thousands that I have seen.

I remember a woman with multiple sclerosis who was barely able to hobble around with two crutches. There were several periods of time when I visited the city where she lived. Whenever I saw her I was able to actuate her will to be well, to the point where we would dance the Charleston together; in fact, the dancing actuated her will more than anything else we did. She would then throw away her crutches and walk almost normally. But soon after I left she would sink down again, to rise up after I had returned and reactuated her. I realized it was my will for her wellness more than her own that was making the difference. This is not a cure.

A woman was diagnosed as having severe myasthenia gravis, and thymectomy was recommended as her only hope, drugs having failed. One day she came to the realization—she described it as a blinding flash of insight—that she had the power within herself to cure herself. She stopped her medication, in spite of medical protests, and started an active program of visualization, and she furthermore completely confounded her doctors by taking up running. Some ten years later she was still completely symptom-free—all because she raised her Life Energy, rekindled her will to be well.

There were two men with amylotrophic lateral sclerosis, a fatal disease. One resisted all efforts on my part and others to activate his will. He told me quite bluntly that he just wanted to survive thirteen more months, because if he were alive then he would come into a large sum of money which he had left for his wife in his will. If he died before that, his widow would receive nothing. He died thirteen months and a few days later. He measured out his desire to live so very accurately and tragically.

Then there was the other man with the same illness, who when I saw him was in a far worse physical condition. He had given up his work and spent his days watching television, smoking, and drinking beer, waiting to die, wanting to die. He stayed but two or three days with me, and this time was devoted intensively to actuating his will through music and other acts of Creativity.

Soon after that his footdrop, which had prevented him from even walking well, had virtually disappeared and he was able to start running. He has confounded his doctors by remaining alive and continuing to run some ten years later. And of course he stopped smoking and drinking— for, at last, he wanted to be well.

Here is an example from today. A friend called me yesterday to say that she had an infection and asked if there was anything I could suggest to help her. I responded by sending over some nutritional supplements. I called today—I called her, she didn't call me—to ask how she was. Worse, she told me. "Didn't the supplements help?" I asked. To which she replied that she had been too sick to go downstairs to take them. Whatever the diagnosis of her infection may be, the underlying illness is her loss of the will to be well. This I call the Inner Flame problem.

I like to imagine that each of us has an inner flame burning inside, almost like a fireball of passionate enthusiasm for life. But all too frequently an event occurs which is taken negatively, which is perceived as a trauma. And this has the effect of, as it were, turning down the heat of the inner flame.

This occurs many, many times to us throughout our lives. Nearly always the flame quickly burns bright again. But sometimes it does not, and now we are in a state of lowered Life Energy and we are predisposed to illness. And every illness has what I call a particular disease diathesis, a particular aspect of the Inner Flame problem that is specific for each chronic illness. So to really cure a serious illness, the inner flame must be reactivated generally, and also specifically in terms of the diathesis for that particular illness. For only when the will to be well is strong, only when the Life Energy is high, can true healing take place. Only then can there be Creativity: the best choices consciously and unconsciously for health, for life, and for love.

With the technique of Life-Energy Analysis (see page 123) one can determine the precise trauma that caused the Inner Flame problem, and then, by invoking Creativity, turn it around and transmute it into the wholehearted embracing of life.

You may be wondering about death: there are high Life Energy deaths. For example, on his deathbed, blind and knowing he would never rise again, Bach composed his highest Life Energy work, BWV 668, "Lord God, I stand before Thy Throne."

And Blake, it is said, sang exultantly "Songs of Joy and Triumph." An eyewitness wrote "he died . . . in the most glorious manner. . . . Just before he died His Countenance became fair. His eyes Brighten'd and He burst out into Singing."

If a person has no will for himself to be well then he cannot have it for anyone else.

The mother of an autistic, brain-damaged, neurologically impaired, blind boy calls to cancel her appointment to learn how to help him with his abject suffering. She can, deep in her heart, want what is best for him only when she wants it for herself. Before she can help him, she must first overcome the Inner Flame problem that has haunted her since the tragedy of his birth.

Over the years I have investigated and researched a large number of patients and clients in both my own practice and those of many other practitioners in many different areas of the healing arts. In at least ninety percent I have found that there is an Inner Flame problem, the will to be well is reduced.

And even if there appears to be no illness, it may often be a question of time, for the diathesis has been established, the negativity is working. So whatever the practitioner does, if it is really to help the sufferer, it must first actuate the will. In fact, to do this and nothing more is very often quite enough. Once the Life Energy is flowing, once the Healing Power is actuated, the body itself so often makes the right choices for health and life.

Furthermore, I have found among practitioners, as with their patients, that about ninety percent of them also have an Inner Flame problem. And this prevents them not only from relieving it in their patients but also from even diagnosing it. The rekindling of the inner flame must be the primary aim of the practitioner, for himself and his patients.

The object of our search is the fire of grace
which enters into the heart.

— THEOPHAN THE RECLUSE

FOLDING THE TENT

No more will, no more soul, no more life!

— George Ohsawa,
the founder of Macrobiotics

When the desert nomad, his habitation becoming no longer life-sustaining, decides to move on, he folds up his tent in a definite, preordained manner.

And so it is for the sufferer afflicted with a grave illness. He too is now a nomad, lost in the wilderness of despair. And there are, for him too, definite preordained stages for the folding up of his tent of life.

The first is the Inner Flame problem. As a result of a specific psychic trauma, he turns down his inner flame of life, greatly reducing his Life Energy, and thus predisposing him to disease—which one depending on his specific disease diathesis.[17]

It is as if he says to himself, "If this is what life is all about, then I don't want it. I don't want to kill myself, but death would be good."

Very often the precipitating trauma is a rejection, in some way, by someone of the opposite sex. All of us have suffered numerous such rejections. And they soon pass, the inner flame again burning bright. But the one time that it doesn't flame up leads inevitably, in time, to the second fold of the tent.

Now the poor sufferer believes that he is programmed to die of a particular illness—and often on a day of high significance for him, for example, his wedding anniversary or mother's birthday. This programming, of course, further reduces his Life Energy, thus greatly reducing the prospects of cure.

The tragedy of this stage is that it is nearly always initiated by a doctor, most often the one who first gave the dread diagnosis. So much more could be done here by teaching doctors how not to do this, for the giving of the diagnosis should be done in such a way as not to destroy all hope. Quite the contrary!

If this stage is not corrected, it leads inevitably to the third fold—and this seals his fate even more. He has now entered a stage of extreme denial as the only way he can find to avoid the horror of the suffering he fears lies ahead.

He now so deludes himself that he believes, unconsciously, that his physical body is immortal. No disease, no catastrophe can in any way harm him. "If a train ran over me and cut me up into little pieces, my physical body would be unharmed."

In this deluded state, he gives up all attempts to overcome the disease. He need do nothing, for his body is immortal. And now his Life Energy is so low that no inner healing can occur, and the later inevitable folds will be made, inexorably. He will wander off alone to his death in the wild.

With each progressive folding, treatment becomes more difficult, for the sufferer contributes progressively less Life Energy to his recovery. But even if new wonder drugs and operations do "cure" the disease, they will not empower him to reerect his tent, once again to make his Home on Earth. He remains a lost soul.

And this will only ever be overcome with therapy to alleviate the suffering of his soul—by soul therapy.

THE EGO-LESS HEALER

THE TREATER MAY RELIEVE the symptoms but, at the same time and as part of the same treating process, may destroy the remaining vestiges of the sufferer's aspiration for Health.

The True Healer cares little for symptom relief as such, but is instead vitally concerned with the sufferer's aspiration for Health, for Life, and for Love. For, unlike the treater, he himself has such aspiration.

And again unlike the treater, the True Healer can accept what appears to be failure, for it is not his ego he believes which brings about the cure.

Only a True Healer can ever be ego-less—truly altruistic.

The therapist recognizes
the sufferer's
Thusness,
but the treater
only his own
me-ness.

EACH ACCORDING TO HIS LIGHTS

... so many years of fearing death.

—SHAKESPEARE

ONE DOCTOR EXAMINES my body and, according to his lights, finds certain abnormalities that he then proceeds to correct. Another examines my blood and, according to his lights, proceeds to correct the abnormalities his system has revealed.

If they are wise, they look not just to the abnormalities but also to their patterns: what they tell about my underlying malfunctioning that has produced them. And then they attempt to treat not only the abnormalities *per se,* but also the causative underlying patterns.

But how far do they go in discovering the basic pattern, the particular disturbance in the Life Energy, the Spirit, that is the original cause of all abnormalities?

For example, a disturbance of the metabolism is revealed to the doctor by certain biochemical tests of the patient's blood. He makes a diagnosis of hypoglycemia, and then, according to his philosophy, prescribes for it naturopathically or allopathically. And if he is wise, he considers the broader pattern, the patient's pancreatic function, his hepatic and adrenal status, his overall nutrition—and more.

The holistic chiropractor, according to his lights, will come to a similar diagnosis, not by blood tests but through a pattern of particular musculoskeletal abnormalities. And then, in keeping with his philosophy, correct the bodily abnormalities and also prescribe naturopathically.

But they both need to go further—to correct the underlying psychopathology of spleen meridian problems, for the spleen meridian supplies Life Energy to the pancreas.[18]

Nor would it be enough for the acupuncturist to treat only the meridian disturbance. He needs to know that the negative emotional state of the spleen meridian is a lack of faith and confidence in the future.

And they will then need to go still further, to the underlying spiritual problem: that the sufferer does not believe in his mother's love, does not believe that her love will always be there, whatever happens to him in life. This I call the *safety net syndrome*.[19]

His basic spiritual suffering that leads in the end to the bodily disturbance is a lack of faith in the Mother, in God. Rather than the grateful acceptance of his life's course, there is instead a fear of the Way.

And underlying all fears of the future lurks the blackest fear of all—death.

This the Healer, whatever his profession, can discern—must discern—from whatever tests he performs according to his lights.

Whatever his particular philosophy, this he must address to really aid the sufferer.

THE PATIENT AS A "LAUGHING CLOWN"

*Now I let myself be ruled once again by the laws of nature alone,
and she has restored me to my original health.*

—ROUSSEAU

WHEN I WAS YOUNG, there was a fairground amusement game called the Laughing Clown. It consisted of a bust of a clown with its head tilted back and its mouth wide open, as if it were laughing. The idea was that you pop some ping pong balls into the mouth, which would go down the gullet of this clown and then come out into a transparent stomach. If the balls landed on certain numbers you won a prize.

It often seems to me that this is a good analogy for what is called orthodox medicine. But it is really an analogy for much unorthodox medicine, too. In a way, it represents what the treater—as distinct from the therapist—does in his practice. The treater is the one who just says to the patient, "I know. Open your mouth and take what I give you." And whether he is giving a chemical or food supplement, or a homeopathic remedy, the attitude is still one of treatment, not of therapy. Not assisting the Life Energy, but imposing something on it.

I used to look at these so-called Laughing Clowns and never understood why they were called laughing, because, although their mouths were wide open, they weren't smiling. What was obvious (although I didn't have the word for it then) was the orality of the whole situation. A better word I'd have for it now would not be the laughing clown but the gullible clown.

This is what the patient wants—and this is what the treater gives. "Tilt your head back, and open your mouth. I'll pop these white things in, and you swallow. And if we're both lucky, they'll hit the jackpot."

THE WATERSHED EXPERIENCE

WATERSHED: A CRITICAL POINT that marks a major change of course; a turning point.

A mountain range is one of the boundaries of a watershed—it can be raining on one side and bright sunshine on the other. How to help the sufferer cross over the ridge?

Many years ago, I met a world-renowned pianist sorely afflicted with cancer. I offered to do anything—everything—to help her. Most of all, I suggested that I would rent a cottage by the sea and work with her, be with her, for as long as it took for her to turn herself around—to embrace Life. She arranged to come at the end of her concert tour, but she succumbed before then.

Ever since I have been obsessed with the idea of therapy as a watershed experience: the sufferer staying as long as is needed to bring about a permanent change.

Until he can proclaim, with the deepest conviction, I will never again be as I was before. I have passed the turning point. I have crossed over the ridge. I am changed—permanently. I embrace Life. I am ready to walk out into—run out into—the sunlit Garden of Life.

There must be no time limitation—but rather, a stay for however long until the critical point has been passed. Perhaps a few hours, perhaps . . . who knows? And all the time working towards this permanent change. With the strongest intention.

The sufferer must set out with this strong intention. The journey to the therapist must be like an odyssey. His goal always clearly before him—want to change. I will change.

All the things that I do are designed to help the sufferer cross over to the sunlit side. And I try to make even a brief contact at least a mini-watershed.

HOW LONG DOES A SESSION LAST?

How long does a session last?
How long will it take you to change?

A MOUNTAINEER ASCENDS the steep face step by step, hammering a piton firmly into the rock to support him for each step on his progress. Piton by piton—each one secure, so he will never fall back.

How long will it take?
It depends on the mountaineer and the mountain.

How long will it take me to ascend to the top?
It all depends on you and your mountain.
Just concentrate on making each step a secure, permanent change.

GETTING THE MAN IN TO FIX IT

A PSYCHOANALYST WHO had been a Spitfire pilot gave this analogy of disease and treatment.

He said that when you pulled out of a steep dive, the compass needle initially gyrated wildly from side to side, but usually eventually came to rest in the new direction. But if the pull out was too extreme, then the needle jammed, and "you had to get the man in to fix it."

The gyrations coming to rest is the Homeostatic Principle in action; the jamming occurs when this is no longer enough to overcome the disturbance—it is outside its range of correction.[20] Now outside assistance is required. And this can be of two kinds, each a different man being called in to fix it.

If the jamming is extreme, then all the wonders of modern medicine and surgery must be employed, and thankfully. This is calling in the treater.

But so often all that is required is a very skillful nudge or tap, to just the right place on the compass with just the right direction and velocity. This is the therapist.

Like a skilled fender repairer, he carefully surveys the crumpled fender and, if there has not been too much jamming, strikes just once in exactly the right spot, and suddenly, almost miraculously, the fender pops back into shape, "cured."

This is therapy, not treatment. The difference is that, unlike treatment, the therapist knows that the compass, the fender, the sufferer, wants to be normal again—has the Homeostatic Principle. It is This that is jammed.

And so often all it takes is a skillful nudge to get It working again. This is the beauty of the subtlety of therapy.

WHY DO WE HAVE EMOTIONS?

IF "EVERYTHING WE HAVE has a purpose," even the lowly misunderstood appendix, then why do we have negative emotions? What is the advantage for us to have the ability to feel, for example, unhappy or sad?

The answer lies in the very word *feeling*—we feel them. And the feeling being unpleasant should then motivate us to move out of it, by transmuting it into the positive—happiness or joy. And then this pleasant feeling tells us our work is done. It gives us positive feedback.

This would be the Innate Intelligence, the Homeostatic Principle, in action. If it is unsuccessful, then "the man must be called in to fix it."

VI.
MAKING POSITIVE CHOICES

---◦◄●►◦---

THE DRIVE FOR LIFE

Human nature is disposed to do good,
as water flows downwards.

—MENCIUS

THERE ARE SO MANY procedures and techniques, systems and modalities, all proclaiming themselves as therapy.

They are entitled to do so only if, whatever the means whereby, they raise the Life Energy, the Healing Power within the sufferer: if they raise the sufferer's will to be well, if they enhance his Life Energy.

All spiritual endeavors have as their supreme aspiration the attainment of Perfection. It was Dogen, the great Zen master, who significantly modified this: the purpose of our aspiration is not to become Perfect, to acquire the Buddha nature, but to realize that we already are Perfect, that each of us is a Buddha. Each of us is already a Buddha—we just have to realize this, realize it deep in our hearts.

It is my belief that each of us can find this Perfection in ourselves only when we first find it in another, in the most significant Other, in our mothers: to go deep within her and find the All-lovingness, the Beloved-ness, which is her deepest self, her soul. Once we find it in her, then and only then can we take it into ourselves, introject it. This is a very difficult task, which few accomplish. Perhaps it can be made a little easier.

Let us start by abandoning words such as Perfection, Buddha nature, God within, and so forth. They are all so emotionally charged, and very frequently activate a negative response in us because they seem so unattainable. I ask you to go deeply into your mother to find her Perfection, her Soul, her Belovingness, and you scoff, resist, and turn away defeated. But what if I use another expression which is more acceptable, apparently more mundane? What if I ask you just to go into your mother and see the workings of her Maternal Instinct? With this you will be far more comfortable.

But you will still protest that many, many of her actions toward you were hardly manifestations of the Maternal Instinct—in fact were perversions, even reversals of it. This is true for all mothers. This I refer to as the ego-misprocessing of the instinct. But nevertheless, you can readily see through the misprocessing to the pure Maternal Instinct which has driven her throughout your life. So it becomes easier by this means to find the Perfection in your mother, because that is what the Maternal Instinct is.

But now how to find it in yourself? All of us have a Maternal Instinct—for it is but one manifestation, one aspect, of the Life Instinct, which of course we all possess. This Life Instinct is what Freud called Eros.

Bruno Bettelheim writes this about Eros: "It was our love for others, and our concern for the future of those we love, that Freud had in mind when he spoke of 'eternal Eros.' The love for others—the working of eternal Eros—finds its expression in the relations we form with those who are important to us and in what we do to make a better life, a better world for them."[21]

This is the Maternal Instinct, this is the Love Instinct, this is the Life Instinct which we all possess. When we know this deep in our heart's core, then and only then will we enter what the Buddhists call the Free Land—only then will we find Heaven on Earth, for only then will we know the Perfection which is each of us and everyone—and especially our mothers.

But the use of the word "instinct" in this context leads us into ethological considerations which were not Freud's intention, for, as Bettelheim points out, Freud was very careful not to use the word "instinct," in German *instinkt*, but instead used *trieb*, which means "drive." So he wrote not of the life instinct but the life drive (nor of a death instinct, but of a death drive). Bettelheim goes on to point out that the word "instinct" was chosen by the English translators in an attempt to make Freud sound more scientific, in the same way they translated the German word for soul as "mind"—more scientific but, tragically, less humanistic.

Here are some of the synonyms for drive—force, pressure, urge, impetus, impulse, thrust, motivation. This is what Freud had in mind: this force, this energy arising deep within us, driving us into life, into love. It is this that I mean by the phrase Life Energy.

And this Life Energy, this life drive, this Eros, is within us as our deepest motivating power. How can we not then see that we all are Love, that we all are Perfection? Every moment that we fail to realize this is itself a manifestation of what Freud called Thanatos, the death drive. But here I disagree with Freud in the sense that I do not believe that the death drive is as deep or as important as the drive for life. Thanatos only exists because of our misprocessing, our misperception of Eros.

Now to come back to Dogen. The purpose of all spiritual endeavors is just to reduce our ego-misprocessing that we may find Eros within us, and thus live accordingly.

How can you not believe that your mother has a maternal drive, a drive for Life? And how can you not believe that you have, too? All we need to do is to hold on to this belief and to make it ever stronger and take it ever deeper.

LIFE AS AN EXPERIMENT

All life is an experiment,
the more experiments you make the better.

—EMERSON

EMERSON SHOULD BE PLEASED with me. I've changed countries five times and my practices innumerably. They change with me as I evolve—and the joy of my work is that I can immediately incorporate into it any change within myself. For my practice is me.

Each change is a new experiment. And for each of them I am eventually grateful—although, at first, my faith is often tested. The transitions have become easier since I came to realize that every experiment is always successful—once we give up setting hypotheses.

The words *experiment* and *experience* are related, having as a common ancestor the Indo-European root *per*, to try, to risk.

To try, to take the risk,
is to experience life to the fullest:
an ongoing experiment
which is always successful,
when there is faith and trust,
and gratitude and courage
—the Thymus Attributes.[22]

POSITIVE CHOICES

Only when we are sick of our sickness, shall we cease to be sick.

—LAO TZU

EVERY CHOICE FOR LIFE, for health, for love—if made for the right reasons—will lead to another, and to another, escalating geometrically. In but one day of only positive choices you can ascend so high!

And the place to start is with nutrition: choosing not what "tastes good" but what "does good." The sufferer who complains that health-giving food "tastes bad" has yet to make the choice for health. And until he does, the suffering will continue.

At every moment throughout our lives we are at a fork along our path. Will we choose health and love—or not? There is always the choice.

A FELLOW TRAVELER

SOME YEARS AFTER HER husband's death from bowel cancer, I asked the widow (I can't say "his" widow, for the dead have no possessions, not even widows) if she had noticed any early signs of the developing malignancy.

She stated that for three years before it was diagnosed she had noticed, almost daily, traces of blood in the toilet bowl. She suggested repeatedly to him that he see a doctor, but he always refused. And he became progressively angrier with her, demanding that she stop nagging.

Eventually he did go, but by then it was too late—and he achieved his wish to die.

Why did she stop nagging? It is not because she didn't love him, but because, in the end, she too succumbed to his desire for death. That occurred at the very moment when she was forced to choose between domestic quasi-peace or his life.

This happens within the families of every sufferer with a serious chronic illness. A time comes when they, too, capitulate to the disease. The wife gives up preparing healthful food for her cardiac cripple. He pushes it away and demands the foods they know he should not eat—and in the end she surrenders, as he already has done long ago.

She ceases to fight the disease for him and becomes a fellow traveler.

But as soon as his Will to Live, his Desire for Life, is actuated she can at last minister to him, lovingly.

Alone, the load is so often too heavy. She, too, needs help to want health—health for him.

The holistic therapist must always be thinking of the whole family—for all True Therapy must be family therapy.

THE SUFFERER AND HIS FAMILY

I ask you for no reward in return, except love towards kinsfolk.

—KORAN, 42:22

I SUGGEST TO A WOMAN whose husband has just had a heart attack the foods that can most help him. But she protests that he won't eat them, he doesn't like them.

What would he prefer? The sensations from his taste buds (perverted as they are)—or life? And anyway, will he really not eat them? A man will do almost anything for his wife if she "sells" it to him in the right way. It is very important that she, too, wants life for him.

A similar story: I was consulted by the sister of the head internist of a major hospital. He had just been diagnosed as having inoperable cancer, for which his colleagues had "given" him but a few months more of life. Was there anything I could suggest, his sister inquired, reminding me of how orthodox her brother was.

At that time a book had just come out written by a doctor in a similar situation who had saved his life with a macrobiotic diet. So I suggested that she give him a copy of the book, and to make it more "palatable" we highlighted just the few paragraphs that he really needed to read.

But he did no more than read the blurb on the back jacket before throwing it angrily across the room at her, screaming that it was heresy. Stating in the most definite and final terms that he would sooner die as an orthodox than live as a heretic.

However, the sister prevailed on his (much younger) wife, and they hatched a plan to tell him that he was not eating macrobiotic foods—heresy!—but just Japanese food. And this he willingly ate for some weeks. However, this plan came to nothing when his wife, for reasons that I can only surmise, one day felt that "out of truth" she should tell him that it really was macrobiotics. Of course he refused to eat it ever again. If memory serves me right, the wealthy widow soon remarried a much younger man.

The importance of these stories, and so many others I could tell you, is that it is essential that not only the patient, the sufferer, want to get well, but so too all his family. For every illness is a family problem, a mutual spiritual crisis. We do not suffer in a social vacuum.

THE MOMENT OF TRUTH I

Look in thy glass, and tell the face thou viewest,
Now is the time that face should form another.

—SHAKESPEARE

IN A BULLFIGHT THE MOMENT of truth is when the poor bull, so persecuted, so tormented, so exhausted, can no longer move. So depleted of all pride and anger that he can no longer even lift his head. And he sees right before his eyes the point of the sword that is about to end his life. This they call his moment of truth, but it is really his moment of death.

We too have a moment of truth, but it can be instead a moment of life. In fact we can make every instant of our existence such a moment of truth, such a moment of life. Or not—as we choose.

Like the bull, we too are exhausted by a life that seems to be a never-ending fight. We have tried attacking, we've tried running away. But now let us stop, before all of our Life Energy is dissipated, and stare right at the point of the sword and see the precise nature of our suffering. And then invoke the Power that we all have to make another choice, to embrace Life. All it requires is the courage to have insight.

THE MOMENT OF TRUTH II

Vitam impedere vero—to devote one's life to the truth.

—JUVENAL

SOME YEARS AGO I WAS consulted by the manufacturer of a large range of health products. To health, health for everyone, he proclaimed his dedication, loudly and apparently proudly. But there was a disharmony, a dishonesty, between his public proclamations and what he felt in the privacy of his own heart. This he knew, although he would not openly reveal it, albeit just to me. And this was the cause of his suffering, which was so obvious as to be almost palpable.

He did acknowledge, finally, that there were problems with the formulations of many of his products, and that in some ways they may actually be doing more harm than good to those who took them. This is what I call a partial—almost—moment of truth.

The real moment would come when he had to decide whether he really was a businessman interested mainly in making money, or an (almost) altruistic health provider, which is the image of himself that he was "selling."

I told him that I felt that it would be fairly simple to change the formulations to improve their efficacy. With this he was obviously happy. But—and here was the moment of truth—if I could not improve certain of them, and if, as he realized now, these were likely to be doing more harm than good, would he still sell them?

At that moment I lost him.

In the years since then I have deeply regretted being too confrontational with him. But my question was meant to be not the end of our consultation but rather the beginning. My therapeutic aim was to help him over his fear of the future, his fear of letting go, his lack of trust. To encourage him to have faith in his future, not to be dominated by the fear of a possible loss of income but rather to embrace gratefully whatever lay before him. For there are no traumas—only blessed events which, tragically, at the time are seen as traumas.

Had he had the courage, the trust, to stay one minute more with me—had he faith in our future together rather than in only the next few minutes—I think I could have helped him to cross over. To go past his fear and to then truly make his products a gift for the health of man, which he now claimed with his mouth, and which he would then also believe in his heart.

But no moment of truth is ever wasted, ever ignored, whatever its origin—crisis, storm, or confrontation. And so I am not surprised to hear through mutual friends that since our meeting he has changed, and so have I, for it was also a moment of truth for me—as they all are. I hear that he is less money-oriented, less ambitious, and happier. And also it is common knowledge that his products have improved.

The difference between us was only one of phase. He believed that on the surface he was interested in health, but underneath his primary motive was money. Whereas I believed in the opposite: that his primary motive, his deepest intention, was altruistic, selfless love. He believed that I had an even lower opinion of him than he did of himself, whereas the opposite was true, and I wanted him to embrace my belief.

VII.
THE STUDENT

—◦◦◦—

STUDENT OR PATIENT?

*Our work is to promote change
and we can only hope that such may occur.*

—WALTER CARRINGTON,
the great teacher of the
Alexander Technique

WHEN A THERAPIST, as distinct from a treater, has difficulty with a sufferer it is often because the sufferer is still a patient, not yet a student. He has yet to want to be well. And so, wanting to continue to suffer, he resists the therapist's attempts to help him out of his suffering.

So the therapist is fighting both the patient and the illness.

I can recall numerous patients who, when I suggested that their present doctor was not helping them—in fact, they were obviously dying—would not hear of another referral. "But he's so kind, so understanding." Yes, he'll kindly hold their hands—as they die. Never an argument, never a disagreement—"so understanding." But the doctor never confronted the patient's wish to die. He did not understand at all!

I am reminded of a Marx Brothers film where they are defending Margaret Dumont from an attack by bandits. Groucho quips, "We're fighting to save this woman's honor—and that's more than she's ever done."

No, the therapist can't fight the soul disease and the patient. The first step in therapy must be to actuate the sufferer's Will to be Well, turning him into a student. Allies.

WHY THE WORD "SUFFERER"?

Why do I use the word *sufferer*[23] rather than *patient*?

A patient dissociates himself from the healing process—he wants the healer to do it for him, like leaving his car with the mechanic. He turns the therapist into a treater. Whereas a student wants to be taught how to heal himself.

Both the patient and the student are sufferers, for, as the Buddha taught, all our lives are suffering. Hence the one word suffices for both. However, the sufferer who is aware of his suffering and wants to overcome it is not a patient but a student.

Why the word *student*? The word is derived from the Indo-European root *steu*, "to push." From this is derived the Latin *studere*, "to push on," and *studium*, "application, zeal."

The student zealously pushes on to learn. So, unlike the patient, only the student ever graduates out of suffering.

THE DIAMOND IS MOST REFRACTIVE

The sufferer's distorting ego
so deflects his inner light
that he can no longer find
his way.

The diamond is the most refractive
of all substances.
And, if held just so,
it will redirect the beam,
the sufferer now walking
into his own light
focused ahead of him.

MAKING THE VOW

When the blood burns, how prodigal the soul
lends the tongue vows.

—SHAKESPEARE

A VOW IS THE MOST sincere, solemn promise.

The dedicated student makes a vow to learn all he can to actuate his Life Energy. And his therapist makes a complementary vow to teach him.

This mutual vow is at the very heart's core of all True Therapy. Without this bilateral, equal, and total commitment there can never be True Therapy.

And the task of the True Therapist, the Holistic Healer, is to help the student make such a commitment—and, of course, to make it himself.

One definition of a vow is: "a solemn promise to live and act in accordance with the rules of a religious order." And in a sense, this is what the Therapeutic vow is: to live, as best as possible, in accordance with the rules of Health, Total Health. And to undertake this commitment with all the fervor, the enthusiasm, and the passion, as if it were the rules of a religious order. To make a wholehearted, total commitment for Health, for Wholeness for oneself, and for All.

Few students make such a vow, and just as few therapists.

But there is more to the definition, for a vow is also a declaration. It needs to be, must be, expressed in words—and strongly. Not just said, but declared. And no therapist encourages such a declaration from his student or makes it himself.

But why not?

Let the therapist declare to his student his vow to teach, to heal, to his utmost limits; and let the student declare to his teacher his vow to learn, to be taught, to his utmost limits.

For both of them, this mutual vow can be itself the greatest Therapy.

A vowless therapy
is merely treatment.

Why not make the vow to dedicate your life to Health, to Love?

We all have resistance, ambivalence, to these highest ideals. The purpose of the vow is to stiffen our resolution. A man reluctant to make a marriage vow has not yet made the decision to be faithful — a part of him still wants to fool around. And not to make a vow for Health, Total Health, means that the sufferer is ambivalent—a part of him still wants to be ill, still wants to suffer.

So once again the problem is the diminution of the Will to be Well, the turning down of the Inner Flame. And the primary task of the True Therapist, as always, is to help the sufferer actuate his Life Energy, to have his Inner Flame burning bright.

Now he is prepared to make the vow. Now his ambivalence is dispelled. Now all of him wants to fully embrace Life.

Now he is the committed student, filled with enthusiasm.

Now the therapist can really teach him—can show him all the Beauties of Existence: help him to feel, to know, the omnipresent Numinosity, to ultimately realize, like Emerson, that every experience in our lives can be—is—Epiphanic.

All this can be taught once the student vows to want it—and if the therapist has himself made the vow.

The perfect teaching situation is the True Student and the True Therapist each delightedly showing the other his newest Discovery, his latest Revelation.

THE RIGHT REASON

Renunciation of objects, without the renunciation of desires,
is short-lived, however hard you may try.

—SWAMI NISHKULANANDA

SUPPOSE THAT YOU ARE a severe diabetic who hasn't eaten any refined sugar for years, because it is not on your diet. And further suppose you come to know that tomorrow you will die. Knowing that this is your last day ever, will you eat candy, or ice cream, or cake—or all of them? What can it matter? You're going to die anyway. At last, you can indulge yourself!

Would you? Patients say "Yes!"—but students "No."

I recall a woman with such severe colitis that she was threatened with the removal of most of her bowel. Her illness disappeared after I placed her on her right menu (which she saw as a diet, as a restriction). After a year of unprecedented good health, she demanded to know when she could go back to eating "good" food. So she was obviously still a patient.

A patient does what is right for only a superficial and limited purpose. Whereas the student does what is right for no other reason than because it is right.

JUST HANGING AROUND

THE BEST TEACHING is done not in a formal setting, but informally—the less structured, the better. Not in a classroom, but just sitting around with your teacher, or going on a walk with him. Or watching him work.

I learned much more observing my medical teachers in their practices than they ever taught me in their classes. And this is certainly how I learned psychiatry—not the theory, but the practice of it. By hanging around with my mentors.

And years later, when I wanted to learn of herbalism and psychic and spiritual healing, I hung around some great healers—living with them, eating with them, playing with them, walking with them. Often literally sitting at their feet as they worked and as we talked.

This is the best system—learning by osmosis. Just being there, over an extended time, and soaking it in, almost unknowingly. Not taking notes. Not taking down the words of the teacher, but absorbing his essence.

And this is how I would like it to be with every student who comes to me. No formal, structured sessions, but us just sharing time together. Just hanging around. But however casual it may appear to be, we are both ever-mindful of the reason we have come together: to help him embrace Life, our mutual therapeutic intent.

TWO WHEELS ON DRY LAND

To find health should be the object of the doctor.
Anyone can find disease.

— A. T. STILL,
the founder of Osteopathy

MANY YEARS AGO, when I was the chief psychiatrist in a hospital, my task every morning was to examine and diagnose the patients admitted the previous day. They were then seen by the head psychologist, with whom I would confer over lunch.

I will never forget what he said to me one day. He complimented me on how brilliant my diagnoses were: "You can smell a delusion, you can ferret out a hallucination, but"—and this has always stuck in my mind—"did you know that this woman grew prize camellias? Did you know that this man played the piano?" "No," I replied, a little bemused, "I wasn't trained to find the good things."

But from then I started to, and ever since I have looked for the good things. What the patient *can* do, not what he can't. His deficiencies and his weaknesses are so obvious, but his strengths, tragically, are deeply hidden: that is what makes him a patient, a sufferer. For it is his strength alone that will alleviate his suffering.

Some years later I was taking photographs at the seashore just before dawn. I backed my car into an area of what seemed to be dark grass but which was instead a deep waterhole. The car started to rock back and forth precariously. At any moment it seemed it would slide into the water and me with it. I managed to ease my way out and jump onto the land, and then walked some miles until I eventually got a tow truck. The operator merely attached a hook to the front of the car and in a minute or so it had been rescued. Then he made a remark that still resonates with me as powerfully as the psychologist's: "It's a good thing that you had two wheels on dry land."

That, I realized, was the patient's strength: the two wheels he still had on dry land. Medicine, on the other hand, concentrates on the two useless wheels submerged in the dark water. That's what I've been trying to do increasingly since the psychologist's admonition: to concentrate on the two wheels on dry land, on what the sufferer can do.

This is his Creativity. This is the Power within him that alone can cure him. This is his innate ability to make, at every moment, the best choice for health and love and life. And this Creativity springs from what we might call the Muse, the Healing Power within, the Innate Intelligence—there are many metaphors for It. And every act of Creativity actuates the will to be well and enhances the Life Energy.

When this is actuated, the sufferer who comes before the practitioner is transformed from patient to student. A patient demands that the practitioner do the work. He acts as if he were taking his car to the garage. He is uninvolved in the treatment process, as if he were asking to be called when the repair is finished.

A student, on the other hand, takes responsibility for his suffering. He doesn't want treatment but tuition, knowledge. He asks enthusiastically, passionately, for more information, for more that he can do to activate his Healing Power so as to bring about his own true cure.

> Patient:
> Rx—*recipe* [Latin]: take thou.
>
> Student:
> Fx—*facio* [Latin]: I do.

With the student, there is a cooperative partnership with mutual gratitude: a student grateful to his teacher, the teacher grateful to the student for allowing him to release his healing instinct, to be his teacher of self-therapeutics.

And there is so much to teach, so many ways in which one may enhance one's Life Energy. But the greatest teaching, that which most actuates the student's Creativity, is through music and the other high creative arts. When taught in very specific life-enhancing ways, these, more than any other modality, can best get the whole car back onto *terra firma*.

Pity the poor psychiatrist and his patient. The psychiatrist programs the patient to bring the "bad things," and that is all his patients ever give him. However high his Life Energy may be when he starts work in the morning, and it is very unlikely that it would be high, it is certainly down within the first few minutes of the first lamentations of the first patient. And if, by some most unusual circumstance, the patient does come with his Life Energy high, and thus comes more as a student, he will not survive even the first minute of the psychiatrist's own negativity. They are both locked into the "bad things."

As an ex-psychiatrist, I am still at times surprised that a student will come to me and tell me of his "good things," that he wants to continue to learn from me how to do them even "better," how to be ever more Creative. So many times at such moments I have given thanks to that psychologist and that tow truck operator.

> *The new image of humanity emerging in our century*
> *is that of the divine artist in everyone.*
>
> —JUDITH CORNELL

JUST ANOTHER ORTHODOXY

And every Generated Body in its inward form
Is a garden of delight and a building of magnificence.

—Blake

SOME TIME AGO I HAD the opportunity to become a partner in a very large and successful preventive/alternative/complementary medicine practice. I decided against it after a meeting with the medical director. In fact I came to this decision within the first minute or so when he seemed almost to hasten to proclaim to me that he didn't "believe much in psychology" or in the patient's will to be well.

If we have to divide the patient into body, mind and spirit, then he was concerned only with one of the three sides of the triangle. He was just as squarely medical as the orthodoxy that he believed he was setting himself against. His chief purpose seemed to be to create another orthodoxy of his own.

It was still a strict adherence to the extremely limited, and yet so grandiose, medical model. I, the all-knowing, have diagnosed your illness and now will impose the appropriate treatment on it, on you. All you have to do is to eat my manna.

I looked around his office. The patient's chair—perhaps deliberately uncomfortable so that they would not take up too much time—was on the other side of a wide desk with many books and papers intervening. All to reduce the humanity of the relationship.

And there was a small, extremely uncomfortable examining table that was obviously not suited for doing any physical work with the patient. So not even the body side of the triangle was being addressed—any physical contact was merely for diagnosis. He wouldn't even have known how to treat with his hands. It was all done by prescription, mainly of vitamins—less harmful and more beneficial than drugs, but nonetheless still a prescription, in keeping with the medical model.

And, underneath it all, the aloof grandiosity: I know. I tell you. You do what I say.

Over the succeeding years I saw quite a number of his patients, and patients they always remained, for he never encouraged them to be students, to take responsibility for their recovery with him as their teacher. None of them wanted to be healthy; they were still as dispirited as when they first went to see him. None of them had an awareness of themselves and the deeper and most important etiological factors in their illness.

They may have been relieved of their immediate symptoms, of their apparent illness, but underneath they were unchanged, if not worsened, by the clinical experience. I mean that in particular they were given no sense of their own power; it was the doctor and his power that produced the cure. They were but children, treated as children. Worse—as eunuchs—they themselves had no power, for whatever power they may have had was taken from them as the doctor's was imposed onto them, into them.

I remember him boasting that he had beaten a patient's cancer ("the big C")—not that he had helped the patient's Life Energy to overcome it, but that it was only through his efforts, his power.

I can never forget the young doctor who stood with one elbow on the mantelpiece of the lounge in the hospital where we both worked. As he majestically exhaled his cigarette smoke and expanded his arm in a godlike gesture, he proclaimed that it was only he that was keeping his patients alive. There would never be a touch of healing from his hands, his voice, or his heart.

If this is alternative medicine, to what is it the alternative? It is alternative to, contrary to, in opposition to, the Healing Power within every sufferer.

And should we use the word *medicine* at all? For as long as we hold to the medical model we will never think primarily of utilizing the patient's strengths, of activating or, more accurately, actuating their own healing powers.

True complementary medicine is complementary, facilitatory, even exhortatory, to the work of the Life Energy, the Spirit, the Healing Power within.

Whatever the name of the clinic may be, if it is to be any more than just another form of orthodox medicine, it must devote itself, humbly, with the deepest respect, to what Hippocrates called the *vis medicatrix naturae*, the Healing Power of Nature that we all possess. For it is this and only this that can ever bring about a true cure and not just amelioration of symptoms. And however big the clinic, may the doctor be grateful for the gift of being able to be of service to the totality of the sufferer—his body, mind, and spirit.

THE PATIENT'S ENVY

THIS IS NOT A PLEASANT page to write—but I must, for it is very important.

I once had the responsibility of having to tell the patients of a psychiatrist that he had committed suicide. Naturally, many became upset—but nearly as many smiled, and some even laughed.

I was shocked to realize that what they had wanted was not for themselves to become mentally well but for their psychiatrist to go insane. They were envious of his sanity and wanted to destroy it.

How much of their sessions with him, I wondered, had they spent (unconsciously) trying to drive him crazy? And were they doing the same with their families? Were they envious of their sanity? Trying to drive them crazy rather than helping themselves back to normality?

And what of my patients? Were some of them envious of my sanity and trying to drive me insane? A sobering thought—and valid.

I saw their envy back then all those years ago, but I did not know how to overcome it. Envy is so intractable, Bacon declaring that it ceases only at the grave. In this instance, the doctor's grave—so the envious patient hopes.

How many times have I heard a patient say, smugly, that he is still alive but his doctor dead. No pity, no sorrow, no compassion—he is pleased. Like when he hears that his psychiatrist's own marriage has failed.

The envious patient wants his doctor's death, wants his marriage to fail. The envious patient with a serious illness looks at his doctor, apparently healthy. His primary wish is not to get well but to give his illness to the doctor. At best, a therapeutic stalemate. The envious patient looks at his dentist's healthy teeth. His drive is not to have such teeth himself but for the dentist's to become diseased like his.

For him to succumb to this envious wish is easier than doing the work to heal himself. And whatever he does do will be done half-heartedly, devoid of zeal.

It is obviously essential to overcome the patient's envy. But how?

Notice that in all the above I have used the word "patient." There's the answer. Patients are envious, but students, thankfully, are grateful.

THE HOT POTATO

This is as difficult to write as the last chapter and, being related, is equally important.

The patient with a serious illness regards it as being like a hot potato. He believes that someone, whom he will never forgive, gave it to him—and he now wishes to pass it on, as it was to him. Like a contagion.

This is most obvious with sexually transmitted diseases, but it is there with virtually every illness.

I recall a healer who could not—would not—stop smoking. I was asked by a fellow healer to help him—he did not himself ask, as he had no desire to stop. Nor even the desire to be helped to get the desire to stop.

He told me he had never smoked until ten years previously when he was ministering to a man about to die from lung cancer.

"One last cigarette," he implored. "Please light it for me." Which he did.

Then the fatal words: "And please have one with me."

The healer, in spite of himself, gave in to the patient, who died before finishing his cigarette—and the healer kept smoking. He wanted to—had to—take on the cancer, which the patient had wanted to pass on to him.

I heard recently that my efforts of fifteen years ago had failed, as have those of many other healers. After a quarter of a century, he is still smoking, still wanting to take on the cancer, still "possessed."

Once again, the answer is to help the patient become a student.

The patient does not believe he has the Power to help himself. And for this reason, he wants to dump his illness on another—as he believes it was similarly dumped on him. It may well be that he does not possess enough Power to overcome the physical disease, but he certainly can transcend it: he can heal the suffering in his soul.

And it is this that the student most wants to learn.

GRATITUDE I

Gratitude is a fruit of great cultivation.
—SAMUEL JOHNSON

A VERY SOFT, GENTLE, kindly doctor who really cared for her patients told me that she didn't feel right charging for her work as it had been a Gift to her. So instead she was going to put out a collection basket and accept whatever her patients chose to donate.

I heard that not long afterward she killed herself. At the end of the first week there was only ten dollars in the basket. So she walked out into the sea.

I never expect gratitude[24] from a patient, for only students' hearts are open.

GRATITUDE II

A DOCTOR FRIEND TOLD ME that he had been in an accident that required extensive facial repair under local anesthesia.

What were you doing while he was operating on you? I asked.

I was so grateful. I kept sending him love, for I know how much a doctor needs it.

VIII.
LIFE ENERGY

---※◈※---

WHAT IS COMPLEMENTARY THERAPY?

To COMPLEMENT MEANS to complete. So complementary therapy is a much better term than alternative, for it is not attacking orthodoxy but rather completing the other's deficiencies, adding another dimension, bringing completion. As the *Oxford English Dictionary* defines it, "something which, when added, completes or makes up a whole."

So my work as a complementary therapist is not meant to replace any present treatment. I do not see myself as being a doctor of medicine in the usual sense. I do not diagnose, treat, or prescribe for any particular disease—although my role is certainly concerned with "the restoration and preservation of health." Not the treatment of disease *per se*, but rather the achievement of positive health by activation of the Life Energy, the true Healing Power which we all possess.

This Hippocrates called the *vis medicatrix naturae*, the Healing Power of the nature within us. All of my efforts are directed toward activating this Power, rather than, in the more medical sense, imposing external ones. That is to say, seeing suffering as an internal problem, not an assault by a foreign enemy. Seeing suffering as being the result of an imbalance and a diminution of the Life Energy.

To help bring this about, I work with and suggest many modalities, none of them medical by the more orthodox definition, for example:

dietary advice and nutritional supplementation, many physical procedures with the body, acupuncture, affirmations, and meditations, among many others.

I, of course, employ the techniques that I have developed with Life-Energy Analysis to determine the precise level of Life Energy and the particular blockages to its flow through the body and the ways these may be most easily corrected. And there is tuition on the many ways in which the student can himself raise his Life Energy.

In particular, I encourage a more positive outlook on life and a deeper and broader philosophy of health and healthy living. I concentrate not on the negatives, on the deficiencies, but on the strengths, on the positive attributes.

To do this we—the sufferer and I—work with activating the Creativity, so that he can learn to make the best choices for growth, for health, and for life. Creativity, more than any other factor, will most raise the Life Energy, will most activate the sufferer's own Power to heal himself.

Although I no longer practice orthodox medicine, I am still very much a doctor in the sense of being a teacher. And I see the sufferer not as a passive patient but as an active student, thirsting for knowledge, yearning to learn how he can help himself. He takes responsibility for his own present situation in life, whatever it is, and comes to me as a student requesting tuition on how he can raise his Life Energy to overcome his suffering.

I believe that all of our problems are basically spiritual in origin. The only real solution comes about through an activation of the Spirit, the deep desire for health and life and love. I would like the sufferer to see that his central problem in life is spiritual, as is mine. And I would like him, to the best of his ability, to make a commitment, a dedication of his life to the highest values. I do not expect him to always be in that state, no more than I am. But I ask him to make a commitment to work for it, for it to be his goal.

As you can see, very little of what I outlined takes place in most orthodox medical practices. I try to complement, to add to what the sufferer may already be receiving.

My goal is to assist him in raising his Life Energy by teaching him how to actuate his inherent drive for Life and Health and Happiness.

> *He that hath light within his own clear breast*
> *May sit i' the centre and enjoy bright day.*

> —MILTON

THE ACUPUNCTURE SYSTEM

When you can love without constraint, you maintain a balance
of force that keeps your mind and body and spirit functioning
and moving in a direction for growth and development.

— ROBERT FULFORD, D.O.

THE ACUPUNCTURE SYSTEM is constantly working to maintain a balanced
flow of Life Energy, *chi*, throughout the body.

Moment after moment this balance is disturbed by all internal and
external events—thoughts, desires, actions, all physiological activities,
walking, talking, standing—and every environmental factor. All impinge
on the Life Energy of the organism. The function of the acupuncture system is to monitor these changes and attempt to correct them, thus maintaining homeostasis.

This ongoing, never-ceasing process is unconscious and automatic,
but it can be greatly assisted by acts of Creativity, which not only can correct the disturbances but can increase both the quantity and quality of
the Life Energy, our essential possession.

LIFE-ENERGY ANALYSIS

The healer within can be approached from without.

— GEORGE GOODHEART, D.C.

LIFE-ENERGY ANALYSIS AROSE out of my own development of the system of Applied Kinesiology originated by Dr. George Goodheart.[25]

It is Life Energy that causes us to grow and heal and love. It flows throughout the body via the acupuncture meridians, each of which vitalizes certain organs, muscles, and tissues.

In addition, each meridian has a specific emotional attribute associated with it. And this is the link between mind and body, the basis for an understanding of psychosomatics: each organ and muscle has, as it were, a particular emotion. When the Life Energy is flowing freely throughout that particular meridian then the emotional attribute is positive, and the associated organs and muscles and tissues are healthy. But when there is trauma, of whatever nature, then the emotion turns negative and the Life Energy flow is impeded. If this remains uncorrected, disease results.

Furthermore, many points on each meridian relate to a very specific psychological, and hence physiological, aspect of the particular emotional attribute of that meridian. Thus, by determining an imbalance at any of these points, a very precise physiological and psychological diagnosis can be made, including the precise nature of the particular traumatic event, present or past.

Then very specific measures to correct the imbalance at the point may be instituted by a variety of modalities—nutritional supplementation, physical corrections, acupuncture, particular affirmations, musical motifs, songs, etc. So by being able to pinpoint the precise traumatic event, a choice can then be made to release the emotional blockage, enabling the Life Energy once more to flow freely.

But this work of Life-Energy Analysis, although extremely helpful, is still based, in part, on the medical model of diagnosis and treatment. There is a more holistic way.

It has been found that the most basic meridian problem of all is that of feeling unloved by one's mother. When this is overcome, most of the Life Energy problems previously manifest are automatically corrected, this state of Belovedness so enhancing the flow of Life Energy. And this is the way of High Creativity, especially Music, True Music.

REFINING INTUITION

TODAY I HEAR (or better, feel) the cello's A string. Yesterday I felt the suffering of the woman before me. And both had the same problem.

The string has gone "dead," as happens eventually to all strings, and to all people. And, in a sense, the woman too has gone dead: she has felt dead inside, she later confides, ever since the abortion many years ago.

I know that the string and the woman both have the same problem, for they both arouse the same feeling in me: that I have suddenly become dead inside. I know this because this particular feeling (and so many others) has been induced in me so many times by so many sufferers.

> *... one's whole being vibrates like strings brushed*
> *by an invisible wind.*
>
> —PETER RUSSELL

There is a profound electromagnetic quality to the meridians and their therapeutic use. This use is simple, it is done by hand with one's hand and one's mind and one's heart.

—GEORGE GOODHEART, D.C.[26]

THE TRAGIC PARADOX
OF HUMAN EXISTENCE:
THE NEGATIVE INVOCATION OF LOVE

Many people seem to live "in character."

—H. G. WELLS

EACH ACUPUNCTURE MERIDIAN has a concomitant positive and negative emotional state. And many of the points on the meridians (possibly all of them) relate to specific subdivisions of the major emotional attributes. The negative attribute of the gall bladder meridian is that of rage. And there is one point, one aspect of rage, which particularly relates to Gall Bladder 9.

I refer to this as the Acting point, even better would be the Hypocrisy point. We each lead a lie of a life, acting as if we are loving people and yet believing in our hearts that the very opposite is the case. And each of us has a particular charismatic character whose own public persona we try to act the part of—Mother Teresa, St. Francis, the Virgin Mary, among many others. We act as if we are loving saints yet believe that deep inside we are evil.

When a situation is presented to us which seems to challenge this false persona, the response is one of rage, specifically Gall Bladder 9. There may not be any outward expression of rage, but nonetheless, that negative emotion has been invoked and is having a negative effect within.

Unbelievable as it may seem to our conscious selves, just to think of love, of spirituality, of God, and so forth, or even to hear, let alone speak, these highly emotionally charged words is enough to challenge our acting and invoke rage in response.

Furthermore, should the situation persist, it will lead to a deterioration from rage to hatred. To put it oversimply: to say "love" (with meaning) once or twice may briefly invoke Gall Bladder 9 rage, but to repeat it (meaningfully) twenty times will lead to hatred, and this more negative state will persist far longer than the rage.

So, every time that I have suggested and encouraged someone to love his wife, his children, nature, the flowers, the scenery, whatever, there has usually been a positive superficial result. But I have come to realize that I actually increased his suffering, for now, albeit unconsciously, he is more afflicted by hatred than when he came to me for help. The invocation to love has produced the opposite result. And this I have found over the years with many people.

I can speak of the Will to be Well, or of Life Energy, without raising in you resistance to it. But should I say that this comes about through the opening of the heart, then I have caused it to close down even more!

I used to encourage musicians to act on Beethoven's prayer, "From the heart may it go to the heart." Sometimes it seemed to work, but nearly always, on deeper examination, the hatred would appear and, all too frequently, would become manifest, if subtly.

My findings show this to be so common that it is, I believe, perhaps the main reason for the failure of virtually all spiritual teachings. Even if the teacher himself does not have the problem, he will still almost certainly activate it in his student. But all too tragically, the teacher himself suffers from the same problem, thus further compounding the negativity, the basic contradiction of his conscious intention.

I have come to realize, like Freud and Jung and virtually all the great philosophers and healers and teachers whose works I have most admired, that the root cause of human suffering is a problem of the soul. Yet, if I introduce that word, as I have now done with you, it will activate (I hope but momentarily) a Gall Bladder 9 problem.

Read the teachings of the Buddha, of Shinran, of Dogen or Lao Tzu or the Bible or any of the hundreds of similar books and you will be mentally uplifted—but underneath no longer just a suffering seeker but now one also imbued with negativity. Such a challenge are these great works to our false persona, to our acting.

Superficially you may feel better, but all of my research for many years into this rejection of love shows that deep inside there is more of the un-spirituality, of the soul distress, that brought you to seek help for your suffering in the first instance. You may believe that you have been made more loving, but what has most likely happened is that you have reinforced your acting, deluding yourself that you are even more like St. Francis than you believed before.

Delusions destroy life, for there can be no healing and no growth without truth, without reality. And the truth of it is that in our hearts we really are all saints, just as saintly as whoever your character is. There is only what I call ego-misprocessing that prevents us realizing, as Dogen taught, that we all are Buddhas, that we all are Perfection. (And now I may well have activated Gall Bladder 9 in you once again.)

I believe that the only real cure to human suffering is the recognition of our own Perfection (beware Gall Bladder 9!)—to recognize that we all are Spiritual Beings (GB9!). This is, after all, what the great teachers have always taught. But how to come to this realization, this Truth, without invoking rage and hatred? Controversial as it may seem, all the practices of meditation seem to invoke the negativity. And so do all religious activities. Whenever there is the invocation to love, we are so threatened that we go into hatred.

So how to arrive at our goal, the alleviation of suffering, "spiritual enlightenment" (GB9!) without causing the very opposite? The answer, I believe, is similar to play therapy with children, the play being used by both the therapists and their little patients as a metaphor for the "real" world.

The best analogy I can think of, and it is not a good one, is the way to approach a skittish horse: offer the oats with one hand, the other holding the bridle hidden behind your back. Let us not take the analogy too far— the point is that we have to find a way of reducing the fear of exposure of one's believed evil in order to prove to him that his fears are groundless, just ego-misprocessing, for truly he is Perfect, he is a Buddha, he is a Spiritual Being (GB9!).

This I call Aspirational Play, and of all the modalities I have used in my practices over the years, this is the one I love most, for I believe it is the highest of them all, as it most easily achieves our higher aspirations.

For it is so seemingly just fun, just pleasure. It is play, <u>but</u> play with purpose, play with an aspiration, play with Aspiration—although we do not talk too much of the aspiration lest that vitiate its realization. It is singing and dancing and drumming, it is making music in so many ways. And it is using all of the creative arts—poetry, prose, painting and drawing, photography and sculpture—for Creativity comes from the Muse.

Not just singing and dancing and painting, but doing it in those special ways that will achieve our aspiration seemingly unknowingly. It is only when we have achieved the first step on our journey of Creativity that we then look back and see the unstated Aspiration that directed us. Only when we have found the Buddha nature, the saintliness, the God within (use any metaphor you may choose, but be aware of Gall Bladder 9!), only then can we safely invoke Love and know that It will appear. And only with Love, with Belovedness and Belovingness, can there ever be a true alleviation of the suffering of humankind.

ASPIRATIONAL PLAY

We ought to dance with the rapture that we should be alive
in the flesh, and part of the living incarnate cosmos.

—D. H. LAWRENCE

Her father has just been murdered, and she is as you would expect. I do the usual psychotherapeutic things—and then I mention music. Suddenly her eyes brighten, "I used to play the castanets."

So I show her my collection. She very carefully chooses one particular pair. Then she starts to play. And with the intensity, the poignancy, and the passion of one who is suffering deeply. Her face lights up and breaks into a big smile. She is starting to again embrace life.

It is not just a diversion, for there is love, there is peace, and there is gratitude.

She had asked me for a psychology book to help her cope with death. I show her several—and also one on the castanets which is the one she chooses. She leaves with her book and her castanets. Tomorrow we will work just with them. And through the play I will try to impart to her a philosophy of the acceptance of life, and death. It will be play, but much more—play with a higher purpose. This I call Aspirational Play.

*Above all, it is the will for progress
and self-purification which lights the fire.*

—THE MOTHER

THE DISEASE DIATHESIS

thinking makes it so

—SHAKESPEARE

THE WORD *diathesis* MEANS a predisposition or tendency to a certain state. A disease diathesis is the particular precondition that renders a person liable to a particular disease. I have found that for most serious diseases there is such a diathesis — a specific desire for a particular illness which long predates its clinical appearance. Of course, this desire for the illness is not the only factor that causes it.

The origin of every disease is multifactorial, but nonetheless, I believe that this is the most basic etiological factor that must be corrected. Any therapy that does not eradicate the desire for the illness can never be a true cure, only ever symptom relief. In fact, it could be argued that the desire for illness is its first and most basic manifestation—it does not lead to the disease, it is itself its core.

And furthermore if the diathesis, the desire, is corrected before clinical manifestation, then true prevention has taken place.

As an introduction to this concept of disease diathesis I have decided to use amyotrophic lateral sclerosis as an example, mainly because the diathesis seems to be fairly simple to understand.

As I have delineated in my book *Life Energy*, each acupuncture meridian has a particular positive and negative emotional attribute. With the liver meridian it is happiness and unhappiness. We feel happy when fortune—lady luck, our mother—smiles on us.

And one particular point on the liver meridian is related to a very specific state of unhappiness: a yearning to be reunited with the mother and the doing of some activity, or in a sense the non-doing, so as to bring this reunion about. In amylotrophic lateral sclerosis it is the liver meridian which is involved, and specifically the yearning for mother which is Liver 7.

I first found this problem in a young woman from Canada who had been working in New York without a work permit. She had fled her home as a teenager when her sadistic father punished her by forcing her hand onto an electric hot plate. It was not so much this that traumatized her and caused her to flee, but the look of acquiescence with his action that she saw on her mother's face when in terrible pain she cried to her for help.

It was now some ten years on and her father was dead. While on a trip back to Canada she decided to visit her mother, and they were reunited. She returned to work in New York with mixed feelings. The Canadian-U.S. border is one of the easiest to cross by car; usually the U.S. Immigration officer just waves you through. This time he stopped her car and apparently just in conversation asked her if she was coming in as a tourist. Instead of merely nodding, she readily proffered that she was coming in to work. "Do you have a work permit?" he asked. "Oh no," she nonchalantly replied. So she was refused admission—and had to return to her mother—all in response to her yearning for her, to her Liver 7 problem.

You can see that it was her action that caused her to be sent home, back to her mother. Her action, and at the same time her inaction—her not doing, her not nodding.

I have found this particular yearning for mother, this Liver 7 problem, in the half dozen or so cases of amyotrophic lateral sclerosis that I have seen. I cannot, of course, say that it is present in all cases, and this is offered more as a suggestion for further research than an empirical fact. Of course there are many patients with a Liver 7 problem who never developed amyotrophic lateral sclerosis—but they all did want to become paralyzed, for they all had the disease diathesis. Perhaps some of them, if left uncorrected, would have gone on to develop it, but I stress there are many, many other factors that also must fit into place for this disease to appear.

Nonetheless, it is my strong suspicion that without the desire for the illness, the specific disease diathesis, it would not occur.

How does this specific desire for paralysis relate to yearning for the mother? It is part of the nature of a paralyzing illness to have to be looked after and mothered, the patient progressively becoming a smaller and smaller child, and then a baby to be nursed until death. In a most tragic way, the yearning for the mother is fulfilled by this most incapacitating disease.

Here is the best example I can give of this particular diathesis. A woman of sixty had been adopted and had therefore spent her whole life yearning for her natural mother. She had (seemingly) coped with this yearning fairly well until she was strongly encouraged to engage a private detective to find her mother, on the off chance that she was still alive, for she would be about eighty. The mother was soon located in a nearby village. Rather than approaching her directly, the woman had her husband, a very astute lawyer, write her a letter, as unthreatening as possible.

Every day the woman opened her mailbox, anxious for a reply, yearning for it. After a week it arrived. She remembered clearly how excitedly she tore open the envelope and held the letter in her left hand—she was very certain of this—as she read the reply. It could not have devastated her more. It read, "Whoever told you about me should have his tongue cut out." Within a week the first signs of paralysis appeared in her left hand.

When I saw her, the paralysis, although now more generalized, was still fairly mild. I held out some hope to her, because this causative factor, which she readily acknowledged, seemed to be so important. But she never came back. Her yearning to be with her mother, now deceased, was too strong.

I recall another victim who was a very wealthy banker. Within a few days, and after many therapeutic modalities, including the activation of the liver meridian, he was considerably improved — for example, now singing and even dancing. Most importantly he was filled with hope, his Life Energy, his Healing Power, was high and so were my hopes, but I had failed to take account of his wife.

In anticipation of his forthcoming death, she had already taken a lover and had made plans for the disposal of all the money that would come to her when he died. It was not in her plan for him to live. So she never brought him back. His yearning for his mother could not be met by her, and so he had to try ever more desperately, becoming ever more paralyzed until death.

The desire for the illness I regard not only as being a predisposition to it but as itself being the earliest form, the *anlage* of the illness.

I have just received a greeting card from a man with ALS I saw but briefly ten years ago when he had been "given" by his doctor only at most a year or two of life. In a short time together we did many things, including music and art, and especially helping him to happiness (liver meridian), and more. When I first saw him he had given up completely, slipping into paralysis, into ever more needful infancy. He spent his days in front of the television set, smoking and drinking, increasingly nursed by his girlfriend.

All that has gone now, all the yearning has gone. In these ten years there has been no progression of his paralysis; in fact, it has considerably lessened. He is now happily married, and his pronounced footdrop, which made it very difficult for him to walk, has now apparently disappeared to the point where he jogs every day. He has done so much for himself to raise his Life Energy, and without even knowing it he has especially helped himself by overcoming his disease diathesis.

There is, I believe, a diathesis, a desire, a predisposition for every major illness. And the true cure, and even more importantly the prevention, will come about only when this is acknowledged and overcome.

Do not love your ill-health
and the ill-health will leave you.

—The Mother

PERSONAL HONESTY

*I grew convinced that truth, sincerity and integrity
in dealings between man and man were of the utmost
importance to the felicity of life.*

— BENJAMIN FRANKLIN

THE BLADDER MERIDIAN is the meridian of peace, of resolution.[27] In regard to this, one of the most important points on the meridian is Bladder 2, which relates to personal honesty.

Until there is honesty, there can never be a cure, for the cure is Truth. Each of us has a part of himself that he keeps to himself, that he will never or only rarely display—"I will not show my true face to the world— just my 'good' one."

However, it is not his true face that he hides but the other face, the one he regards as "bad." But until he brings these two together—the "good" and the "bad"—there will never be peace, for there will never be resolution of these warring factions; they will be ever fighting in him.

The musician who has come to consult me gives a nondescript, misleading, and in fact dishonest answer when I ask him why he has come. It is obvious he is in deep suffering and just as obvious that he does not want to reveal it. It is as if he wants me to intuit the cause of his suffering and relieve it without him experiencing his moment of truth. But this will not work—in fact for me to attempt it would be dishonesty on my part. He tells me of the years of devoted study that he has put into his violin. And now he plays professionally in an orchestra. But what music do you make for yourself? What do you play at home? His answer: "I never play for myself, I only practice for the next concert." But something must have gone wrong. What happened to your devotion, to your love of playing, that now you do it only for professional reasons? What has happened to your love of playing music?

He instantly dismisses what I am suggesting. And yet he knows in his heart that it is true, knows how many times he has wanted to smash his violin, how many times possibly even wanted to cut his tendons so that he would never have to play again—as others like him have done. In him, as in so many others, there is the loss of the love of music—the hatred of music is now the lot of this poor professional. I can do nothing for him as long as he holds onto his dishonesty; only when he reveals this negative side can I take him beneath it to the love that was always there, that will always be there. But first there must be the moment of truth, the honesty.

It will be easier for him when he trusts enough, for he has music, and the easiest way to bring about the resolution, to find the peace, to find the love, is through music. Let it take your hand and guide you down into Her Realm, the Land of Belovedness.

The fear of looking inside is the most irrational fear of all. In the dark the child fears a tiger, but the mother switches on the light and the tiger becomes just a chair. But when, in your moment of greatest fear you turn on your light, the experience will be a revelation, it will be epiphanic. Not just a chair—but the glory, the beauty, the Perfection of you, your Self.

God is here now—and It is You. And all around you, and all inside you is the Heaven of your Existence.

The windmill you are attacking and guarding yourself against is only a delusion,[28] a play of the mind. The disbelief in your own Perfection.

> *The life of every man is a diary in which he means to write one story and writes another, and his humblest hour is when he compares the volume as it is and what he vowed to make it.*
>
> —J. M. BARRIE

But look again at what you have written, it is a bible, your bible. There is a South Carolina mountain proverb, quoted by Artie Shaw, when he was confronting his moment of truth: "We ain't what we wannabe and we ain't what we're gonnabe—but we ain't what we wuz."[29]

But we wuz and are and always will be Perfect.

My ultimate therapeutic aim is to help you realize your Perfection—this is your real moment of Truth. And it is my belief that until you know this Truth deep in your heart, your life will continue to be one of suffering. For all our problems are spiritual—and our only spiritual problem is in not realizing that we *are* Spiritual.

All our problems
are spiritual,
and our only
spiritual problem
is not realizing
we are
Spiritual.

IX.
THE HEALER
AND THE SUFFERER

———✦———

THE VAJRA

All truth has to be expressed in sentences....
The type of sentence in nature is a flash of lightning.

—ERNEST FENOLLOSA[30]

THE *vajra* IS A TIBETAN religious object. It is often referred to as a lightning bolt because it is said to cut through all the delusions that cloud our thinking, to reveal the deep Truth of our existence. For a similar reason it is also called the diamond, because of its cutting power. And to symbolize this, each end of the vajra is diamond-shaped.

In my least humble, most grandiose, and probably self-deluding moments, I imagine myself as such a diamond. Trying to quickly cut through, to dissect, to get down decisively, incisively, to what I believe is the root cause of the sufferer's pain—his spiritual dis-ease.

Over the years I have become increasingly less satisfied with the slower, more "diplomatic" ways of trying to gently ease the sufferer into a recognition of his problem. My chief objection is that the sufferer does not have presented, there right in front of him, what the therapist believes, rightly or wrongly, is his basic problem. For it is only with this direct presentation that he can then be given the opportunity to choose the other path, the way of life and love, and to be encouraged in this by the therapist.

The other way is like peeling an onion, layer after layer, session after session. And so frequently the sufferer (and the therapist) cry before, if ever, reaching the heart.

But with the aid of the diamond he can be given his moment of truth and the opportunity to instantly embrace it.

Or so I delude myself.

THE DIAMOND CUTTER

ONE OF THE VERY GREATEST Zen sutras is called the Diamond Cutter Sutra: the diamond—the hardest substance—cutting down through the illusions to the central glistening priceless gem—our Perfection. Tolstoy called It the God Within; the Buddhists, the Buddha nature.

Whatever its name—there It is! The Diamond of Existence revealed by the diamond cutter.

As I grow older, I have less time for those who want instead a feather. They will be pleasantly stroked—but no Glory ever revealed. And thus no suffering ever relieved.

NOT TO BE A PEARL

I CALLED A PSYCHIATRIST friend in another state requesting him urgently to see an acutely suicidal young woman. He said he would be delighted to—in two months! He was very booked up, he apologized proudly.

What was the sufferer to do in the meantime? I can almost see him shrug his shoulders.

Certainly, there must be a limit to how many sufferers he can see. But can't he rearrange? Can't he postpone the next visit of someone already doing well? I don't mean for him to sacrifice himself, but his practice must allow for emergencies, for those in pain. After all, that should be the main reason he is in practice.

Many a practitioner has what I call a border problem: he will open his heart—but only so far. I find the same in many marriages.

For example, I recall the husband who seemed to be so concerned, so caring, for his very sick wife. But when I recommended one more procedure to help her, he suddenly, surprisingly, rebelled. He would do no more. He announced that he had reached his limit—his limit, not hers.

All of a sudden, in the midst of what appears to be friendship or love, an "iron curtain" descends. "I am delighted to help"—but then the barrier, the closing of the heart—"in two months."

How open can the heart be if it is so ready to close? Love, real love, is limitless, knows no borders, is unconditional—infinite.

So the practitioner with a border problem is never really open-hearted. Why then is this man's practice so busy? Could it be that his patients don't want real therapy, for that demands open-heartedness—and more? However beautiful the pearl may appear to be, it will always be cold, for the oyster can suddenly close.

In their short lives, Schubert composed about nine hundred works, Mozart over six hundred. Reger, Villa Lobos, Bach, and the others—so many compositions! Think of all the books by Dickens, Trollope, Tolstoy, D.H. Lawrence—and the others. And Picasso, Blake, and Turner—and the others.

They were men of infinite creativity, possessed by fervor and passion and zeal. They yearned to compose—they had to! The creativity flowed out of them seemingly endlessly, inexhaustibly. They didn't stop at 6 P.M. They loved to work!

How many practitioners can truly say the same? How many really love their work? Are they working for the work, as the *Bhagavad Gita* teaches? Or for the rewards of the work: the path of routine, of disaffection, of grossly reduced creativity—of cold-heartedness?

For everyone there is a limit, but it should be imposed by the body, not the heart.

And what of the practitioner's family? There must be a limit to his practice time so that he can be with his wife and children, but they must be behind his work, must love it as much as he does. Are they selfless, helping him selflessly to help those in pain—or selfish?

A psychiatrist told me he didn't mind being called at two in the morning, or even going to see the sufferer at that hour. But his wife objected—not for his sake, but for her own. Can he really love his patients if he feels unloved at home?

I used to visit the home of my good friend and first psychiatric mentor whenever I was in his city. We would spend hours talking enthusiastically about psychiatry, and always I could feel his wife's resentment. After one visit, he told me that in the future we'd have to meet at his club, as his wife would not allow me to enter their house anymore. The reason was that when I was last there he had taken a call from a very distressed patient, and his wife complained not about the woman calling, but about him helping her on his day off. "But that's his job," I replied. "He loves it."

It was my last time there. And not too long afterward he killed himself. One main reason, I believe, was that he could not reconcile his love of his work and his wife's hatred of it—and of him, for our true work is our deepest self. He was his work—and, he came to realize, she hated him.

I am blessed that my wife loves my work as much as I do—for so she loves me. She's not a pearl, but a diamond.

MUTUAL BREATHING

As we all breathe together, we become one in thought and being.

—ROBERT FULFORD, D.O.

WHEN I TRY TO THINK of a perfect marriage, my mind goes back to an old couple I knew many years ago. I used to watch them sitting side by side in their armchairs, both gazing silently into the fire. And then, quite abruptly, without a word, both would arise to go to bed—simultaneously, as if they were reading each other's thoughts, as I'm sure they were.

I've always imagined that they were so close to each other that they were breathing in perfect synchrony. Breathing as one.

I often do this when lying beside my sleeping wife: synchronizing my breathing with hers, my soul with hers. It's as if I know what she is dreaming.

Sometimes I do this with a sufferer, and I'd like to do it more. Just sit silently side by side, me synchronizing my breathing with his, breathing sympathetically.

Even better is when we both synchronize our breathing, each reaching into the other, into his soul, to be one with him. Mutual Breathing. The union, the yoga, of our souls.

THE PERFECT BREATH CYCLE

To heal is to bring an individual to a state of wholeness
and well being.
This is accomplished by breath and love.

—ROBERT FULFORD, D.O.

Man has a twofold breathing, one of the body and the other of
the spirit; these two respirations [can] also be conjoined.

—SWEDENBORG

THE CORE PROBLEM of human existence—the reason that our lives are suffering—is what I call the misprocessing of the ego, in which we fail to realize that each of us is Perfection, everyone a Spiritual Being. That each of us in his own uniquely individual way is possessed by the Buddha nature—is a Buddha.

The fetus' first intimation of the Other is the mother's heartbeat and other sounds, but even more so her bodily movements, especially her respiratory movements. Try to imagine being back in the womb, regularly pulsed by your mother's respiratory movements transmitted through the water, pulsating you through the water.

The soul is swayed by the waters.

—CONAN DOYLE

The mother's respiratory movement is the baby's first intimation of the Other, of the Perfection, which he takes into himself. This rhythmic respiratory movement is, as it were, the first transmission from the Muse. This movement is the *anlage* of all dance and all music and all the later, more abstract arts.

All creativity starts with the movement. And perhaps most of the negativity that the fetus feels coming from his mother, which starts the misprocessing problem, also comes to him as the mother's respiratory movement—but disturbed. If the mother is loving the baby, is one with it, her respiration will be rhythmic and relaxed—and loving. And it is this that we seek after the trauma of birth, when on her belly, at her breast, and in her lap, and later throughout life: from her, from others as her, and from music.

And the more we breathe like our mothers at their most loving breathed when we were inside them, the more we will be reminded of their Perfection, and thus find our own.

So I have before me a sufferer, deeply distressed with her life, so much misprocessing that she has no realization of her Perfection, of her Self, as a Spiritual Being. She feels, she confides to me, "amputated from my soul."

I am going to help her breathe as I believe she was moved by her mother's breathing when her mother most loved her in the womb, when she was most aware of her mother's Spirit. I have found that the rate for this is about one respiratory cycle every eight seconds, four seconds in, four seconds out. So initially I move her lower ribs for her in this eight-second cycle. I do this until she settles into the rhythm, and then I let her do it for herself.

After this has become fairly constant, I ask her to stop actively breathing and allow her inner Self to breathe her; not to think, "I am breathing," but rather, "I am being breathed"—by her mother, by her Perfect mother, which is her.

And then I encourage her to hold on to this state of Belovedness through all the vicissitudes of daily life, frequently coming back to the cycle. Attempting to be ever-mindful of it. Impossible—but if only . . .

> If only
> I were aware
> of every breath
> I'm breathed.

I am gradually coming to the conclusion that perhaps the greatest therapeutic benefit of all High Creativity, that is to say True Music and True Art, is to help us breathe as we were rhythmically pulsed in the womb by our loving mothers' breathing, when we felt most Perfectly Loved.

All music, all art,
is primarily movement.

And the primary movement
is the mother's breathing
when we felt most beloved
within her.

But what will I *do?*
the young therapist implores.
It doesn't really matter
what you do,
but what you want
to happen.

Not technique,
but intention.

WHAT DO YOU DO WHEN YOU ENTER?

WHEN YOU ENTER the piano teacher's studio, you go and sit at the piano.

At the drum teacher's, you get behind the drums.

At the singing teacher's, you stand beside his piano ready to sing.

At the art teacher's, you sit before the easel.

At the osteopath's, you lie on his table.

At the psychotherapist's, you sit in the chair.

When you enter my room you could be doing any of these —and more.

DESKS

A healer can't be one
with the sufferer
with a desk between.

The desk also keeps
their spirits apart.

In the dam,
there's ample water,
but none
in the parched valley
below.

All I do
is open
the sluice.

The healer's
raison d'être:
to give
the sufferer
one, too.

Sometimes I just sit silent,
letting the Music inside me play,
and hoping the sufferer hears It too.

Nothing must separate
healer and sufferer,
at any level—
physical, psychological,
or spiritual.

TO BE LIKE CHAUCER

It is said that Chaucer saw deeply
into the follies of human nature.
So do I.

And he felt the suffering.
So do I.

But then a corollary is added:
and he laughed at what he beheld.

I need to laugh more.

TO BE CHAUCER—AND MORE

THEY WERE PROBABLY the most chronically hateful couple I ever tried to treat—back in Australia, many years ago.

In the two years I saw them they both refused to ever come together. They came separately, paid from their separate bank accounts, and separately complained incessantly, each about the other.

I once stopped the wife in the middle of yet another tirade against her husband and asked her if there wasn't anything in all their years together that she had done wrong. Yes, she replied. One thing—I married the bum!

With marital problems I always go back to what I call the first contract: when they each come to realize they are going to marry, although nothing yet is stated. Consider their first contract.

They met at summer camp, and she immediately invited him back to her hut for sex. In the middle of the act, there was a knock at the door— her regular boyfriend had arrived for his share. So she got her husband-to-be to hide under her bed while she then continued her sex with the new arrival. And he, just under them, was really turned on. And so, he said, was she, for he never knew her later to be so vocal and so vigorous.

It was while that sex act (I can't call it lovemaking) was going on that they both, unconsciously, decided to get married!

And now, forty years later, they were seeing me, but always separately, to ventilate their mutual hatred—which also started back then at the moment of the first contract.

She boasted to me that she had had "hundreds of lovers." She maintained a secret apartment to which she brought back any man who attracted her—and she was, as she beamed, "easily attracted."

She'd lean back in my office chair exhaling clouds of cigarette smoke (I let them smoke, back then) and glory in repeating, over and over, "I've had hundreds and hundreds—and all better than him!"

Why not be honest and tell him?

Never, she'd smirk.

And he knew—it was an essential part of their plan that he find out. He used to listen in on her phone calls and open her letters. He had dozens of the most torrid secreted in a safe. And a part of their plan was for him, too, not to tell.

Why not be honest and tell her?

"Never, it's my ammunition for the future." Meaning if they ever divorced, for she had most of the money still in her name. But they never would. They both so loved to hate each other.

Every day there were fights, physical as well as verbal. Often one, sometimes both, would come in—always separately, of course—with bruises, even a black eye. He blamed her for his heart attack and his broken arm, swearing she had deliberately pushed him off the balcony. And she blamed him for her hysterectomy.

Now here's the point of this litany. To the casual observer, they were a sweet, devoted, older married couple. Such was their pretense, oozing charm and affection. But I knew, and had felt, the hatred underneath.

I once had to refer them, together, to an internist for a particular physical illness they had both developed. In his report he thanked me for sending him "such a perfect couple"!

His history and examination, such as it was, revealed nothing of their hatred. Nor did he sense it—or even want to. He made his physical diagnosis, prescribed his physical remedies, and that was the end of his involvement.

That's the difference with a holistic healer. The surgeon never feels his patient's pain—but the healer always. It was because of this that my sensitive, loving mentor in psychiatry killed himself. He could no longer stand to feel the pain of the hatred. For compassion is to share the suffering—to also suffer from the hatred.

Yes, as I've said, I must try to be like Chaucer: to see their folly—and then laugh. And to get them to laugh at their follies, and you at yours, and mine.

Folly implies foolishness, and that's what they are, what we all are. As Dogen taught, we all are Buddhas, but so many of us are foolish Buddhas—too foolish to realize that we are Buddhas.

I—we—need to do more than laugh at our follies. We need to see them as being extreme instances of our misprocessing that prevents us from realizing that we are Love—and are always Beloved.

And then we can laugh—in joyous release, in Ananda—as a saint laughs in rapturous Delight.

WITH OUR EYES CLOSED

With our eyes closed, we can see deeper into ourselves.

—MILTON FEHER,
mind/body dance therapist

I'D LOVE TO SIT by a sufferer, silently, with our eyes closed.

In my years in psychiatry the patients would sit opposite me staring at me, staring into me. Apprehensive, fearful, wide-eyed. All day their staring. I don't think I'm particularly paranoid, but all that staring was disconcerting, and I'm sure it prevented me from doing better work.

Now, thankfully out of psychiatry, I have students, not patients. They don't stare—but they do look at me, all the time. And under their constant gaze, it is more difficult for me to go into myself to hear my Inner Healing Voice.

There was once an occasion when the power failed, but I continued to work in the dark. It was so much easier. Less apprehension—both ways, for I was not seeing them either.

It would be so pleasant for us just to sit together with our eyes closed. This way I could see so much deeper into you, and you into me. This way we can see, know, the other's true Self. And it is then that the highest Healing takes place.

All we need to close our eyes and thus open our hearts to each other is Trust.

Though I do not believe
that a plant will spring up
where no seed has been,
I have great faith in a seed.
Convince me that you have a seed there,
and I am prepared to expect wonders.

—THOREAU

Convince yourself that you have Life Energy,
and you are prepared to expect wonders.

A MINISTER OF THE SOUL?

Man has a Soul which is his real self;
a Divine, Mighty Being.

—DR. EDWARD BACH

THE WORD *minister* IS DERIVED from the Indo-European root *mei*, meaning "small." From it are also derived such words as *minus* and *diminish*. The Latin *minister* meant a servant, and it was formed after *magister*, "master." To minister is to attend to the wants and needs of others, to place oneself at the service of another who is in need, who is suffering.

So a minister of the soul is one who dedicates himself as a humble servant to the soul needs of the sufferer to help alleviate the deep spiritual pain of his existence.

Of his work Freud wrote, "I want to entrust it [psychoanalysis] to a profession that does not yet exist; a profession of secular ministers of the soul, who don't have to be physicians and must not be priests."[31]

Tragically, this did not happen. As I know from my extensive experience of psychoanalysis and psychoanalysts, and its vast literature, it has instead fallen into the hands of those who are concerned not with the soul, but only with the mind.

This was best evidenced by Bruno Bettelheim, one of the few psychoanalytic ministers of the soul, who alerted us that even Freud's use of the word *soul,* which was very frequent, was deliberately mistranslated into English as *mind*.[32] This made him appear less human and denied his spirituality, which his translators themselves felt they did not possess, nor did they want to. Along with this denial of the spirit, analysts have become not ministers but magisters.

Although I in no way practice psychoanalysis, I would like to believe that in many ways my work is deeply psychoanalytically-based. I started reading Freud at the age of fourteen, and ever since he has been deep in my soul. And certainly he was the reason why I chose to practice psychiatry. Let me say a few words about my first week as a professorial intern in psychiatry, one of the only two such positions available at that time in Australia, in the only professorial department of psychiatry then in existence there. Before me lay a very bright future in psychiatry.

In that first week I tried to help a young boy of fourteen who had been admitted to the psychiatry ward with extremely severe asthma, which had already greatly impaired his respiratory function. Several psychiatrists had tried to help him, with no success. I believed that the only answer was psychoanalysis. But there were no medical psychoanalysts in Sydney, and no one in the Department of Psychiatry who was even really interested in it.

So I brought young John into my office, laid him on a small bed (a "couch"), sat behind him, and tried to be a "psychoanalyst." I kept him there for a rigid fifty minutes, during which time he said absolutely nothing. At the end—at last!—I "thanked" him in my best "analytic" manner and booked another session for him.

This time as he lay down on the couch he bared both of his wrists, to reveal a total of five watches, which he then proceeded to stare at— mutely—until the exact fifty minutes were up. At which point I again "thanked" him, and he left.

I should have thanked him, for I had learned that if I wanted to become involved in analysis I had first to be analyzed myself. So in the middle of the academic year I resigned my highly prestigious professorial position and moved to another city, to go into analysis myself. Now, rather than working in a university hospital, I was in the employ of a state mental health department that was so antagonistic to psychoanalysis that had my interest in it, let alone my being in it, been discovered, I would have been removed to a country hospital so as to be unable to continue. Furthermore, I knew that they would then also fail me in my psychiatric board exams.

At that time, the Standard Edition of the works of Freud was being published. I became a foundation subscriber, but I had to ensure that each volume was sent to another address, not to the hospital, lest my interest in—my love of—psychoanalysis be discovered. And I had to keep all of my psychoanalytic books, as distinct from my psychiatric ones, hidden in a cupboard to ensure that none of my colleagues saw them and reported me.

This was not my paranoia, but rather the advice given to me by two other trainee psychiatrists who I discovered, by a most roundabout way, were also in analysis.

Perhaps I can best, and most tragically, highlight the attitude to analysis by the fact that one of my colleagues became increasingly disturbed, and so hateful of Freud, that he blew his brains out over one of Freud's books!

Such was my love of psychoanalysis, and my dedication to it (and especially to Freud). But over the years I became increasingly disillusioned by the magisterial soullessness that I found in it, in its practitioners, and in Freud. Lately, inspired by Bettelheim, I am rereading Freud, and transposing *soul* every time I come across *mind*—and at last I am finding his soul.

It was Freud who wrote, "psychoanalysis is in essence a cure through love." But this I fail to find in psychoanalysts and in their writings. In fact, I believe they want to disown Freud's proclamation, for love is of the soul, not of the mind.

In many ways, although differing greatly in practice, that part of my work called Life-Energy Analysis is based on Freud's psychoanalytic tenets. In fact, a great number of my findings fully corroborate Freud. (I have tried in vain for many years now to find even one psychoanalyst interested in this. I would like them to learn of these aspects of my work which I would offer as a grateful tribute to Freud, but to no avail. Their minds and hearts seem to be closed.)

However close I believe I used to be to Freud, and still am, there are nonetheless some significant differences between my work and his—even allowing that Freud, too, saw the basic problems in life as being of the spirit, of the soul.

One difference is that although Freud wrote extensively about the soul and Eros, still there is a strong impression of pessimism, assuredly relating to his cancer. He seemed to believe that the deeper we go inside ourselves, the more "bad" we will find. I believe, to the contrary, that underneath the superficial dross (which later we will learn is still part of the "good"), there is only Good. I believe that our souls are pure and that all we need to do is open our eyes and see the Glory revealed.

Another difference is that, unlike Freud, I also work with the physical body. For this I am eternally grateful to my teachers, especially Robert Fulford, D.O., George Goodheart, D.C., and Edgar Miller, D.O. Not forgetting the related areas of nutrition, the Alexander Technique (especially Walter Carrington), and acupuncture, to mention but a few of the many modalities which greatly affect the physical body.

Ainslie Meares was the greatest psychiatrist that Australia ever produced. For part of our postgraduate training not only did he lecture us, but we went to his office to observe him in actual practice. Those of us who were psychoanalytically oriented were quite shocked by his physical contact with the patient. In fact, he stated that he learned more about the patient from physically examining him than from the psychiatric interview. He even described in great detail how much he could learn about the whole patient, not just one aspect of his neurological state, by the knee-jerk test. Looking back over the years, I believe that he was trying to teach us about the power of therapeutic touch, for I am sure, now, that he practiced it.

This should have taught me even more, for one of the strictures of psychoanalysis is to have no physical contact with the patients. I cannot remember in six years of daily analysis my analyst ever touching me, except possibly to shake my hand when I met him for my first preliminary interview. It is a long way from no-touch to therapeutic touch, from magister to minister.

Freud and virtually all psychoanalysts seem to have had no contact with the physical, and they seem almost to deny the importance of the body, on both a structural and a biochemical level. And yet, correcting the body distortions releases the entrapped spirit—but only when the physical practitioner recognizes that with his hands he is also a minister of the soul.

This is especially important for me as I increasingly come to realize that our spiritual problems arise from what I call ego-misprocessing of the internal and external reality. And this misprocessing, starting in the womb, is particularly caused by the uncorrected traumas of birth, by the physical distortions of the birth process. When these body distortions are corrected, albeit only ever partially in later years, there is always a great release and alleviation of the soul suffering. For it is only the uncorrected body distortions from birth that prevent us from realizing our Perfection.

I believe that today Freud would as well be practicing what we call bodywork. He would be touching the sufferer, healing with his hands. How he would employ them I do not know, but I believe it would be in a new and most therapeutic way. He would be *actively* healing, not just sitting in a chair. He would use his hands, and his heart, to bring about "the cure through love."

Perhaps the differences between Freud's work and mine could be summed up by saying that Freud did not love music, nor did he feel loved by it.

In spite of these differences, in my less than humble moments, I sometimes believe that although I do not practice psychoanalysis, I may be—perhaps—a member of Freud's new profession, a "secular minister of the soul." Would that this were my calling.

DOES A THERAPIST WORK?

A singer works—
his music is a direct expression of his effort.
But an instrumentalist, by comparison,
does very little work—
he gets the instrument to do it.
His work is in getting it to work.

It's the same with a therapist.
His work is minimal.
All he does
is to get the sufferer's Life Energy
to get on with Its work.

No sweat.

I'D LIKE TO THINK I'M A HEDGEHOG

There is a line among the fragments of the Greek poet Archilochus which says: "The fox knows many things, but the hedgehog knows one big thing"... the words can be made to yield a sense in which they mark one of the deepest differences which divide writers and thinkers, and it may be human beings in general. There exists a great chasm between those on one side who relate everything to a single central vision, one system, more or less coherent or articulate, in terms of which they understand, think and feel—a single, universal, organizing principle in terms of which alone all that they are and say has significance, and, on the other side, those who pursue many ends... related by no... principle. These last seize upon the essence of a vast variety of experiences and objects for what they are in themselves, without, consciously or unconsciously, seeking to fit them into or exclude them from, any one unchanging all-embracing sometimes self-contradictory and incomplete, at times fanatical, inner vision. The first kind of intellectual and artistic personality belongs to the hedgehogs, the second to the foxes.[33]

—ISAIAH BERLIN

WHAT AM I? A hedgehog or a fox?

Here are some of my foxlike activities. Over my years in practice I have worked in General Medicine, Alternative Medicine, and Complementary and Holistic Medicine, as well as in Psychiatry (many subspecialities including child, cultural, and forensic, also psychotherapy and orthomolecular psychiatry), plus my own work of Life-Energy Analysis, Cantillation, and Creativity (including art, dance, music, photography, poetry, prose, and sculpture).

Although I would not name them as such, I have used on virtually a daily basis at least the following modalities: Acupuncture, Applied Kinesiology, Aromatherapy, Body Energy Systems (numerous), Chiropractic, Chromotherapy, Geo-magnetism, Hand Diagnosis, Healing, Homeopathy, Hypnotherapy, Imagery and Visualization, Iridology, Magnetotherapy, Massage, Medical Climatology, Meditation, Nutrition, Phytotherapy, Osteopathy (General and Cranial), Reflexology, etc.

In addition, I bring to every clinical setting my intensive study of at least the following disciplines: Aesthetics, Alexander Technique, Anthropology, Biochemistry, Darwinism, Ethology, Etymology, Folklore, Language, Linguistics, Literature, Oriental Medicine, Pharmacology, Philosophy (many aspects), Psychoanalysis, Sociobiology, Sociology, etc.

All of this would seem to indicate that I am a fox—but do I have an underlying principle that draws them all together, that entitles me to regard myself as a hedgehog?

Monism is defined by the *American Heritage Dictionary* as "the ... view that reality is a unified whole and that all existing things can be ascribed to or described by a single concept or system." Am I a medical monist?

Where to begin? There is no better place than where the Buddha began, with his first Noble Truth: Life is Suffering.

We suffer because our ego-misprocessing prevents us from realizing, deep in our hearts, that there is Belovedness—that our mothers love us; that we are Perfect because she is. That there is a pure Maternal Instinct that we know is her, and this is the "instinct"[34] for Life, for Love. This is what Freud called Eros. And this is in her and all of us. Hence we all are Perfect.

In this grateful state of Belovedness there can be no traumas, only blessed events.

With this soul-knowledge, the Life Energy is greatly enhanced so that at last there is Health. And there is greatly heightened Creativity, because with this reduced misprocessing the ego is now at the service of the Muse, the Innate Intelligence. Therefore the best choices can now be made for health and life and love. And each of these positive choices further increases our Life Energy.

Where does this misprocessing start? In the womb, and then it is greatly exacerbated by the birth process. So the ultimate prevention will be the mother finding Belovedness (the pure Maternal Instinct) in her own mother, for her baby equals her mother.

What can we do now? First we need Insight.

1. My life is suffering.

2. This suffering is my doing, arising out of my misprocessing. And it is my responsibility—not blame, responsibility.

3. I know I have the Power to overcome it.

4. I seek help to learn how to use my Power.

But we can't directly invoke the love/life drive, for to do so actually increases the misprocessing, unconsciously actuating not love but rejection. The answer lies in Aspirational Play, by which means we can find the Perfection, the Belovedness, as it were indirectly, metaphorically to know in your heart the Perfection in a song. Then from there to find it eventually in yourself and in everyone, through knowing It in your mother—as your mother—for music starts with the mother, with her movements, her lilt and her lullaby. And She is the Muse.

Through Aspirational Play, through finding this Perfection in her and in each of us, we become at last grateful adults, and (we hope) eventually sages.

A characteristic of the hedgehog is to roll itself into a ball. I would like to think that I have done the same, rolled up all my experiences. I would like to believe that I am a monist—but anyway I do know I am a "momist."

EVERYONE IN ANY SUFFERING, whatever its type or cause, is entitled to, deserves, treatment to alleviate it. For treatment, suffering itself is the only criterion needed.

But the real "cure" will only come from therapy. And for this the therapeutic criteria must be met.

There is more, much more, to suffering than just pain. Suffering is the soul's sore dis-ease with Existence.

The body is cured if it has decided to be cured.

—THE MOTHER

MY SPECIAL GIFT

> From the heart
> of the Muse,
> the waves of Her pulse
> flow through us
> as Spirit.

EACH OF US HAS a special talent, a gift by which we can best express the Eternal Eros yearning for release.

I try to help each sufferer to find his special gift—and then to make it into his occupation. For only then will he enjoy his labor for its own sake, as the *Bhagavad Gita* teaches. Happy is the man whose special gift can be expressed fully in his daily work.

My late friend, Robert Fulford, in his book *Dr. Fulford's Touch of Life*[35] describes his special gift. His is the gift of touch, of so sensitively feeling the Life Force with his fingers.

What is mine? I believe it is similar to his. A fine sensitivity, not with my fingers but with my feelings. I exquisitely feel the feelings of others—by finely feeling the feelings within me that their feelings actuate.

Let me hear him speak but briefly; let me see him walk or dance but a few steps or move in any way, or sing but a few bars, write a sentence or two, make even a quick sketch. Or let me just look at his face. Let me just feel the feelings that are aroused in me.

I can tell so much about him—by telling you so much about myself: about the me that has become him.

The psychoanalyst Karl Menninger wrote that Jews make the best psychiatrists and musicians because of their heightened sensitivity. This was their gift. I'd like to agree—although not with his patronizing corollary that this is because of their cultural paranoia, arising out of the centuries of persecution. I'd like instead to think it comes from the special gift of the Jewish mother.

Whatever its origin, I believe that this is my special gift: to feel deep within him (and thus within me) the pulse of the sufferer—the way it moves within him, the way it moves him. The way it is expressed in every moment of his life, in every activity—especially his acts of high creativity.

I believe my special gift is feeling, knowing, the pulse—the inner movement. I see and hear and feel, but, more deeply, I sense the movement, the pulsation—of people, of music, of all that emanates from people. Inside myself I move with them. This is how I get to *know* them.

I know how the sufferer moves in the same way I know how "Always" moves, how Irving Berlin was moving when he composed it.

I know how a poem moves—how to sing it. For I know how the poet moved. I move with Turner, and I move differently with Blake.

All is movement, and with all I try to move, synchronously. Not with the superficial gestures, but with the pulse propelling the life movement of the sufferer.

As I move with his pulsation, I start to sense just how this is a distortion of the deeper Pulsation, the Breathing of his Muse. I move to his pulse and to his Pulse, becoming ever more aware of the disharmony between them, their out-of-phasedness. And my work is to help reunite them—to bring the pulse ever closer to the Pulse.[36]

I feel his pulse, I move with it. I sense its irregularity within me, and I then try to help him bring it into synchrony with his Deepest Pulsation, his Muse, his Mother of Love.

This I humbly believe is my special gift. And I am blessed that I can use it every day in my work, as my work.

And I am doubly blessed, for I can, at times, feel the Pulse all around me—in everyone, in all creatures, in all trees, in all music: all the world as Music, Pulsating.

Once divine voices have lost their power to reinforce the human
bonds that create meaning, life is empty.[37]

—JUDITH WEISSMAN

THE DIVINE VOICE is the Muse, the Innate Intelligence, the God Within, the Eternal Eros.

> I help the sufferer
> to find his Muse,
> Who then leads him
> to the Cure.

I'm not concerned
with your disease,
but with the impediments
that prevent you
worshipping Existence.

THE VAJRA AND BELL

WHAT AM I?

I am something of a Tibetan Vajra, the diamond cutter that penetrates through the delusions of the ego to reveal the Truth. And the Truth is always that we are Beloved by our mothers and love her, and all as her, in grateful return. We all are Buddhas—but we are too deluded to know it.

My work is to help the sufferer clear away the mist of ego misprocessing to find his Soul. For this is the basis of all suffering: the anguish, despair, and terror, of the ego, alone.

The guide to direct the sufferer to his Soul must be the Vajra and Bell.

The Tibetan wise man carried in his right hand the straight Vajra, the symbol of his yang power. And in his left, the Bell, his yin. The Bell's roundness, its comfort, its compassion, its mothering, and its Music: her lilt and rocking and lullaby.

The day will come when I will learn to use Vajra and Bell together, when they become for me the One. Then I will, at last, have found my way to help the sufferer alleviate his suffering.

X.
THE FOUR
THERAPEUTIC TRUTHS
AND NON-JUDGMENT

———✦———

THE FOUR THERAPEUTIC TRUTHS

One in All
All in One—
If only this were realized,
No more worry about your not being perfect.

—THE HEART SUTRA[38]

WE WERE TAUGHT in psychiatry that one of the first assessments to make of a patient was of his ego-strengths: did he have the capacity to look inside himself, to develop a true understanding of his inner workings, of his suffering—to develop insight into his true nature?

Only a small percentage of patients would satisfy these criteria and thus be deemed suitable for insight psychotherapy. The others could only be treated more superficially, holding their hands and sustaining them through their crisis, but not being able to help them really understand their lives. For them there could be no real cure, only amelioration of symptoms.

Their lives were suffering, of this they cried, but they seemed to lack the capacity to look at their own contribution to their suffering. They lacked the capacity to go inside and look at what they were doing. All they wanted was symptom relief. This we firstly provided, but then tried to help them increase their ego-strengths so that they would then have the ability to see exactly what their life situation was, exactly what they were doing, exactly who they were, so that then they could rise above the next potential crisis. This I was sometimes able to accomplish, but not very often. The desire for insight, to see things as they really are, is not very strong in most people.

Insight has been defined as the capacity to discern the true nature of a situation, "the grasping of the inward or hidden nature of things"—the inner nature of ourselves and our doings in the world. And we would sooner expend our energies going up into space than going down deep inside ourselves.

While intellectual capacity may be a factor in certain cases, the main reason is our fear of the evil that we think we would find if we did look inside. If we truly believed that we were basically "good," that we possessed the Buddha nature, then we would have no hesitation—we would rush to find It, to embrace It. But tragically this is not so. From our society, our culture, and our religious beliefs, as reflected in parenting, we each have imbued in us a concept of sin, of evil. We believe that we are bad inside.

How many mothers have I heard scream at their children that they were devils—as their mothers screamed at them? Did not St. Augustine teach that original sin was passed on in the womb from mother to child? Very, very few patients come to a psychiatrist without the greatest fear of finding the evil that they believe is inside them, that they believe they are. A few have the courage to face it, for they so acknowledge their pain that they will do anything, even this, to seek relief. Some, just a few, have an inkling that however "bad" they may be, underneath there is the "good," and they are prepared to travel through the evil to arrive at it.

But most people, however great their suffering, fear the psychiatrist because of their belief that he can look into them and see the evil lurking there. This belief is encouraged by the psychiatrist, for he dwells, session after session, on what is "bad" and "wrong" about the patient, never what is "good." So because he doesn't believe in his own innate "good-ness," his Perfection, his Buddha nature—for he, too, is a product of his society—he will never believe it of his patient and help him through his suffering by enabling him to find his own true Self, the Soul.

When, as psychiatry students, we were taught to assess a patient's ego-strengths, what we were unknowingly assessing was the extent of their belief in their own inherent evil. Plus something more: with a few, a belief, or more usually just an inkling of a belief, that maybe there was also sainthood, and also that there was a power (their self-power) that could transmute the evil.

This courage and this faith and trust I call thymus attributes. The thy-mus is one of the master controllers of the Life Energy, of the Healing Power within.[39] Therefore every therapeutic endeavor that raises the patient's Life Energy will increase his thymus attributes and thus his desire for insight. So the higher a person's Life Energy, the higher will be his drive for health and life and love, and the greater will be his capac-ity to look inside. And if it is high enough, there will even be the posi-tive desire to do this. Not, as for most, to do it to overcome his suffering, for that is a negative reason, but instead to find out just how wonderful he is and therefore how wonderful is everyone else.

Everyone has a varying degree of fear about having blood tests. The more confident we are about our health, and the more confident we are that any abnormality can be readily overcome, the less fear there will be. And similarly, the role of the true therapist is to help reassure the sufferer that he need no more fear to look inside than the healthy man to have a blood test. In fact, for both of them it can be a most happy experience.

The essence of the Buddha's teaching is the Four Noble Truths, which may be summarized as follows:

1. Life is suffering.

2. The origin of our suffering is in our ego-desires.[40]

3. The suffering can be overcome.

4. The way to overcome it is through what the Buddha called The Middle Way.

It is the first Noble Truth, that of suffering, that concerns us now. The original word is usually translated as suffering, even better is anguish. So the first Noble Truth for a patient is the recognition that something is wrong, seriously wrong, with his life. That he has anguish, the anguish of the human condition. As one sufferer put it, "The things in my life, the serious things, are not as they should be. And for this I am suffering."

This must be the first step on the path of insight. That I am in pain, life pain. That my cries of anguish are the noisy crepitus of the friction between who I know I should be and what I think I am.

I will give as a random example the last sufferer I saw today, the mother of a severely impaired and autistic boy. I hear from her friends that she is so exasperated, so desperate with him that she frequently screams at him, hits him, and even kicks him. Yet when I ask her why has she come to me, what can I do to help, all she says is that she wants me to write a letter to his school to have him put in a different class. Even though I try gently and repeatedly to get her to talk about what is really going on, she resists every effort.

I don't want her to confess her "evil," but just to admit to her own suffering, the tragic burden that she has to bear. For until she admits that her life is suffering, I can do little but hold her hand. I will not be able to get her to look inside to find the Perfection as the pure Maternal Instinct which is her, and thus I will not be able to help her son to find It in his mother, and then in himself. She must first have the courage to admit to herself, and to her helper, that her life is suffering.

"Where is your pain?" inquires the doctor of the patient who has come in for a physical. But I ask instead, "What is your anguish?"

Only when this first therapeutic truth is acknowledged can there be the start of insight.

The second therapeutic truth is that my suffering is my doing, not my fault—for that again causes us to wallow in evil. It is my doing, and therefore my responsibility to overcome. Furthermore I accept this responsibility.

The third therapeutic truth is that I can accept this responsibility because I have a feeling deep inside myself that I have the Power—I myself have the Power to overcome my suffering.

The fourth therapeutic truth is that I want help to learn how to utilize this Power that I know I possess.

It is the art of the therapist, of the one who desires to help enhance the patient's Life Energy, to activate these four therapeutic truths, for only then can there be true therapy. Only then can the sufferer's own Life Energy be actuated. Only then can there be the true healing from within.

This will come about because the patient (from the Latin *patior,* "to suffer") has now become a student. He is asking to be taught the ways he can overcome his own suffering, for he is taking responsibility for it and thus for its alleviation. Now the practitioner can be a true doctor (Latin *docere,* "to teach"). This is the greatest therapy, teaching the student how to raise his own Life Energy by going deep inside himself to find the Truth of the Perfection that he is.

It all starts with the courage to have Insight.

ACCEPTING RESPONSIBILITY

... that sentiment of responsibility
which is the first step to reform ...

—JAMES BRYCE

THE SECOND OF MY therapeutic criteria is that the sufferer must accept responsibility for his suffering. Responsibility, not blame—for this is judgmental, whether against himself or another. And judgment—"this is good" and "that is bad"—is itself one of the basic causes of human suffering.

When I think of responsibility, I imagine someone surveying a mess before him and pleadingly inquiring who will clean it up. And it is the helper who responds with a "Yes, yes, I will clean it up."

Similarly, the sufferer surveys the mess that he presumes his life to be and puts the question to himself, "Who is going to clean this up?" And he responds, "I will. I made the mess, and now I take responsibility to clean it up, to put my life in order, to overcome my suffering."

There is a deeper meaning to responsibility that is contained in its etymology: from the Indo-European root *spond*, "to pour a ritual libation"; hence to solemnize a promise. Thus, when you accept responsibility for your suffering, when you truly accept that responsibility, you are making a solemn promise that you will devote yourself, dedicate yourself, wholeheartedly and enthusiastically, to learning all the ways that you can most actuate your Life Energy, your Power for Life and Love.

Only in the climate of this promise will we ever live in the Land of Peace.

AM I A MIRROR?

*If I could see in someone's eyes joy and satisfaction
of being with me.*

—ROUSSEAU

MY WIFE HAS ALWAYS maintained that I am a mirror: "something that faith-
fully reflects or gives a true picture of something else." But I am more
than just a passive pane of coated glass. My work, my activity, is to reveal
to the sufferer who he really is. I, as it were, hold the mirror up to his
nature. I hold up the mirror—and adjust it to help him see, at last, his
true nature.

A snapshot is only a picture, but a portrait by a master photographer
is a true picture, going deep within the subject to reveal his inner self, his
true nature.

Initially, the sufferer usually sees his reflection as "bad," for that is
how he views himself. But I try to help him see instead the reflection of
the shining glory that is his True Self—the Beauty, the Belovingness,
which is Him. For this alone is the True picture.

Marvel at this image! Admire it! Wonder at it! (All from the Latin
mirari.)

And remember that these words, like *mirror*, are derived from the
Indo-European root *(s)mei*—"to smile." So look at me—and smile!

NON-JUDGMENT AND PERFECTION

I saw a wicked man ... but in him saw the Power
of the Divine Mother vibrating.

—RAMAKRISHNA

I ABANDONED PSYCHIATRY when I realized that it only dealt with the control of negative behavior and not the activation and encouragement of love. (Note the rarity of the word *love* in the indexes of psychiatric textbooks.) I came to realize that most, if not all, the suffering I saw and felt could be overcome by the patient being in a state of love, for others—and for himself. Self-hatred is a cancer.

But encouraging love was not enough. There was a deeper stage: one can only really love when one feels loved. And this goes back to the mother: when we truly believe she loves us, then we are free to love, and love all—including ourselves and, of course, her.

This root problem of the earliest mother-child relationship is the core of all human suffering—to go through life believing she does not love you (or pretending that she does) is an onerous impediment to vital living. You can never love yourself if you do not first believe your mother does.

The belief in her love, her goodness—however misapplied—must be actuated. This is the central task of life. Only when we can accept her can we accept ourselves, and others, as we are.

This involves the suspension of the crippling judgment we are constantly inflicting on ourselves, and the world. There is no badness, no evil, no sin—just misperception of an ever-elusive reality.

In this state of detachment, of acceptance, of non-judgment, we come to the understanding that all of us are Perfect. And in this state there are no traumata. We accept with equanimity all that comes to pass—triumph and disaster, health and illness, life and death—as The Way.

It is only in this state that the Life Energy—the *chi* of the Chinese, the *prana* of the Indian, the *vis medicatrix naturae* of Hippocrates—can flow freely and abundantly throughout the body, creating the true Health from within. And Happiness and Joy, and the love of Life and gratitude for It.

And will never be any more perfection than there is now.

— WHITMAN

The sufferer hesitantly
opens his heart
and exposes his soul.

See how bad I am,
—and I'm getting
what I deserve.

No—you are Perfect,
and Yes—you are getting
what you deserve.

FRIENDS

We grew together,
Like to a double cherry, seeming parted.

—SHAKESPEARE

WHAT WAS I TO DO with this sufferer? He had flown over from Germany with what I had been told was a "neurological problem."

I was shocked by what I saw. He was in the advanced stage of a progressive, fatal paralysis. He was shrunken and withered, confined to a wheelchair. His legs utterly useless, and one arm also, and there were just a few movements still left in the other. He had lost most of the power to hold his head upright, and his speech was slurred and at first incomprehensible.

I hoped he had not come to me to stop the disease process, let alone reverse it. This I knew in my heart I could not do. But there was much that could be done. We could help him to raise his Life Energy. We could become friends, true friends.

Almost from the very first moment I felt a great sense of trust. Deep down I trusted him and knew that he trusted me. There seemed to be, as it were, no border between us. We spent much time talking—he spoke almost no English and I even less German, so it was all done through an interpreter, our mutual friend.

We talked of many things, and there were long periods of silence when I just sat with him or stroked his body or held his head. But none of this in itself was important; they were all just ways of building the trust, of establishing an ever deeper friendship. And I saw it in his eyes, and I believe he saw it in mine.

We sang together, some German folk songs—and jazz, which he really loved. Every day some jazz friends and I played for him, and he sat in his wheelchair smiling broadly and trying to sing along, gasping— but still smiling. He accompanied us with some bells we had wrapped around his good hand, and by tapping a tambourine that we had mounted in the one place on his wheelchair where it was accessible. And he smiled and smiled—his Life Energy increasing even as his life was running down.

"Ah, jazz!" he would exclaim, shaking and rattling his wrist—and smiling. Jazz was his friend, I was his friend, and so too were the other musicians. And he was ours.

Through this friendship he was set free—free of the fear of the increasing paralysis, free of the fear of the encroaching death. He was free of all the delusions that make life a suffering, whether we are afflicted or not. When we wheeled him out to the taxi to return to the airport, he seemed so tall in his wheelchair—so happy, so free!

Only after he had left did I realize the strength of his friendship, for there was a gap in my life. I missed him. Missed what about him? Then it came to me—his saintliness. I thought that it was my friendship that had made the difference—but it was really his.

A few months later a friend visited him back in Germany. He had physically deteriorated, but his spirit was even higher. "Ah, jazz! Jazz!" he exclaimed, still smiling. "Ah, jazz!"

I heard a little later that he had died, swiftly and peacefully. Death, too, had become his friend.

SUFFERING FROM AN ILLUSION

The shadow of your sorrow hath destroyed
The shadow of your face.

—SHAKESPEARE

ALTHOUGH I NO LONGER practice as a medical doctor, I shall never regret my medical training and experience—from the postmortem rooms of the hospital to the chronic back wards of the mental hospital, which one psychiatrist called the postmortem room of the mind (I would say of the soul).

I have seen, dissected, and examined—and tried to relieve—the most pathetic and horrifying diseases of the body, of the mind, and of the soul. I have known these poor people and watched them wither and die—body, mind, and spirit.

And I have suffered for them. Those dispirited "vegetables" (so they were called) in the mental hospital, who I tried somehow to help more than forty years ago, are still clearer in my mind and heart than any patients I have seen since. The extremity of their suffering brought all of their personalities up to the surface. It was so easy to know them, to really know them—for their souls were open.

At last I have stopped worrying about them—most are now physically dead—but I can never stop wondering. How were their lives after I left? Did any of them ever find Peace? I still wonder, and I always will.

Their suffering, although psychotic, was real. They are the ones who do not cry or complain. Those who do—the great majority of us—are only suffering from an illusion.

FRIGHTENED BY FANTASIES

When I consider life, tis all a cheat;
yet filled with hope, men favour the deceit.

—DRYDEN

WE BECOME DISAPPOINTED when what we anticipated does not come, when our fantasies are not fulfilled. Nearly all our negative emotions—sadness, unhappiness, depression, and so forth—usually arise from mere fantasies we have created.

So many people have a fear of opening their hearts. What are they frightened of? That they may be hurt, they reply. But again that's only a fantasy. In fact, the whole future is only a fantasy. Why fear something that only exists in your mind? Once you realize this, there will be no fear at all, for all fear is based only on fantasy—on what we imagine may happen.

I write this sitting in a cemetery, thinking of the mourners. Most of them are so afraid to accept, deep down, the death of their loved ones that they must create the fantasy that they are still alive, still living at home with them.

It was a horrible experience to see my daughter lying dead in intensive care, artificially "still alive." To gaze on her body, not her, because she was gone—rather to gaze on what used to be her body, knowing that her life was over, for her and for me. I started to cry and then I realized that my tears were for what I imagined would have happened for her had her life continued—what she would have done, what we would have done. Then I realized that I was crying for the non-fulfillment of a fantasy. Crying not for reality—but only for "something" that I had chosen to create in the neural circuits of my brain.

Loneliness is only the non-fulfillment of a fantasy that we have imagined of another at the fireside beside us. Without the fantasy, loneliness becomes peaceful solitude.

Our greatest fear is not of being hurt as we open our hearts, or of loneliness, or disappointment—for underneath them all is the fear of death. It is this fear that activates all the other lesser ones. It is this fantasy that destroys so much of our lives.

And what of the people whom these gravestones signify? When living, they, like us, feared death, but what when they were dying? Did they die in fear of a fantasy, or did they accept and embrace the reality? Perhaps some did. Perhaps at death we all do. Maybe this is the moment of greatest enlightenment, for there can be no true enlightenment when there is fear. Enlightenment is the absolute acceptance of Reality. I do not know what happens at death—not yet.

As long as we fear the fantasy of death we cannot truly enjoy the wondrous beauty of life, for we live in fear of it being snatched away. Can I really enjoy playing music if inside me is the fear of a fantasy that tomorrow I may be paralyzed—or, even worse, die? Can I really love you if I fear the fantasy that one day you may leave me—or die?

What will I do if I open my heart and you hurt me? Notice the *if*— that makes it just a fantasy.

MY LIFE WILL BE REPOSSESSED

If I fear they will come and repossess my piano,
I cannot enjoy playing it.

If I fear my wife will leave me,
I cannot enjoy her presence.

And if I fear death,
I cannot enjoy life.

If you fear
the gates will close
at dusk,
you cannot enjoy
the sunlit Garden
of Delight.

There is a ripeness of time for death.

—JEFFERSON

I received life because the time had come;
I will lose it because the order of things passes on.

—CHUANG TZU

I have been very near the Gates of Death
And have returned very weak
And an old man feeble and tottering,
But not in Spirit and Life—
Not in The Real Man—
The Imagination which Liveth for Ever.
In that I am stronger and stronger
As this Foolish Body decays.

—BLAKE

IN A SENSE, I DON'T care if you don't get better. For I'm coming to realize that we have no way of defining "better."

I do my work as my Muse directs, and I accept whatever happens—to you, and to me.

Perhaps my best work is to teach you Acceptance.

A DIFFERENT VIEW OF DISEASE

Chuang Tzu saw the man-made ills of war, poverty, and injustice. He saw the natural ills of disease and death. But he believed that they were ills only because man recognized them as such. If man would once forsake his habit of labeling things good or bad, desirable or undesirable, then the man-made ills, which are the product of man's purposeful and value-ridden actions, would disappear, and the natural ills that remain would no longer be seen as ills but as an inevitable part of the course of life. Thus, in Chuang Tzu's eyes, man is the author of his own suffering and bondage, and all his fears spring from the web of values created by himself alone.[41]

—BURTON WATSON

NON-JUDGMENT

BEYOND ADJECTIVES lies the Land of Love.

The bladder meridian has to do with peace and resolution—the binding together of the disparate warring factions within us.[42]

A most important point is Bladder 4, which relates to what I call the Basic Split problem: judging everything and everyone as either good or bad. It all goes back to good mother/bad mother, and then on to ourselves—good me/bad me.

It is the harsh judgment of self that readily leads to guilt, and this then prevents us from having the courage to look inside ourselves. If we suspend the judgment, we are then quite willing to look inside—to find that there was no reason to have judged ourselves "bad" anyway.

It is judgment that prevents us from really feeling love. For love is not only non-conditional, but non-adjectival.

> *Recognize beauty and ugliness is born.*
> *Recognize good and evil is born.*
>
> —LAO-TZU[43]

Adjectives activate antonyms. If you say your wife is beautiful, there is usually the implied other side—another woman is ugly. Or, more commonly, at other times your wife is then seen as ugly. The basic split: beautiful/ugly—good/bad.

Your wife, and mine, are beyond adjectives. She is Love—manifested in that special way that is her Self. This unique essence the Buddhists call the Thusness. And this is her Perfection—I use a capital *P* in an attempt to elevate it above the mere adjectival, above the basic split.

When you can suspend judgment, the world changes—in fact, you enter another World.

When you listen to music this way you no longer care if the notes are right or wrong, the interpretation good or bad. You transcend the mundane. You are transported by the music to the Land of Music, the Land of Belovedness.

For the first time ever, you hear Music—not music, but MUSIC. Regardless of performance, composition, or genre, regardless of everything—you hear, you feel, you know Music—and Her Love.

Judge it—and you bring music down to your world, to the mundane. Instead, feel its Thusness, and All is supramundane. All becomes transcendental, epiphanic. Every note numinous.

And as for music, so for life. Feel the Thusness of everyone—the unique manifestation of the Universal Perfection.

> I can only feel
> the Thusness
> of the sufferer
> when I suspend
> judgment of him
> —and his illness.

Beneath the bottoms of the Graves which is Earth's central joint
There is a place where Contrarieties are equally true.
From this sweet Place Maternal Love awoke Jerusalem.

—Blake

WHAT TO DO WITH
A DELINQUENT ORGAN?

our undivided loves are one

— SHAKESPEARE

A CHILD BECOMES DELINQUENT because of a lack of parental love. So the answer must be not to attack him, but to love him.

Delinquent is from the Latin *linquere*, "to abandon." A delinquent account is one which is overdue in receiving money, and a delinquent child is one who is overdue in receiving love—and so is a delinquent organ.

A diseased organ is delinquent—not obeying the normal laws of physiology—because it has been deprived of Life Energy, love. So don't attack it, don't treat it as "bad," but instead give it the Life Energy so long withheld.

Every child, however delinquent, wants to love—and, however diseased, so does every organ.

Try to suspend judgment of the diseased organ. Don't see it as "bad," but just as an aspect of you that needs attention. The loose shingles on your roof that require nailing down are not "bad," only needy.

Do the work non-judgmentally. Just do it because it is there to be done.

XI.
LOVE

---—◦❧◦—---

THE TIME FOR TRUTH

IT IS TIME, LONG OVERDUE, for me to be truthful. All I have written so far is at best half true, and half prevarication, even obfuscation.

I think once more of my esteemed late friend's book entitled *Dr. Fulford's Touch of Life* and wonder about the title, probably chosen by the publisher. I would have liked to call it *Dr. Fulford's Touch of Love*—for that is what he did. I know this because he did it to me many times. As he wrote, "Love is the energy that expresses the physical force."[44]

But *love*, that poor word, has been so imprisoned and abused by religion, which guards it zealously, and so perverted and debased by manipulators, that the discerning public has little trust in anyone who employs it. Often their suspicions are justified, often not. Not with Dr. Fulford.

What about me? I have really wanted to write about love, to try to teach about it.

The parents of a very disturbed child ask me for my "treatment plan" for her. I want to say that I will try to give love to her. But I hold back in fear and instead speak of Life Energy and Creativity. I want to go on to tell them that I want to try to help them give her love. But again I hold back in fear.

What is it I fear? That I will be judged a hypocrite, that they will examine me to find my own areas of failure to love. And that they will accuse me of being a charlatan, a manipulator, a guru (now but a term of insult, implying brain washing).

Why submit myself to this? Better not to use that word *love*. But then I remain a deceiver. I would like—one day—to be like Gandhi: "Truth became my sole objective." But again I retreat in fear. He could say it because he was holy, he was truthful. He had no fear.

All that I can say is that I try to give love to the sufferers who come to me. Perhaps occasionally I succeed. But I always try.

It's very different to say I try to love the sufferers. That's almost acceptable. But it is much more provocative to say I try to give love for this is too active and thus too threatening. For the response against this, the one I fear, arises from the listener's own hatred of himself. He would never give the love, and therefore he attacks anyone who proclaims to give it. Sometimes the attacks are justified, other times not. But they are never justified, even when valid, if they are based on envy.

All I can do is to look into my heart, examine my deepest intentions, and then try as best I can, by whatever modalities seem most appropriate, to give love to the sufferer, that the Healing Power within him may flourish in this climate of safety.

For all healing is initiated—only initiated—in the state of Belovedness.

Love will travel forever.
—IAN DIAMOND

HATE IS JUST THE MISPROCESSING
OF LOVE

Love is a circle that doth restless move
In the same sweet eternity of Love.

— HERRICK

AT LAST I WAS VISITING the office of the psychiatrist whose prolific writings on schizophrenia I had admired for many years. I was shocked by the deadness in his office—and in him. Especially as his writings had seemed so alive, even at times humorous.

He soon confessed to me that he had virtually given up treating schizophrenics: "I can no longer stand their hatred." I confided back to him that I, too, had almost given up treating them: "I can no longer stand the hatred of their parents for them."

My psychoanalyst once told me that for two years he had really struggled to try to treat a young schizophrenic man. At the end of that period, his parents really thanked him for his help. It was then, he told me, that he realized he hadn't helped him at all—for such was the parents' hatred that they didn't want him well.

Hatred by the patient—hatred of the patient. So much hatred in psychiatry! Oftentimes more, much more, than the psychiatrist can bear.

I wish I could go back to those long-past psychiatry days, to try to see the hatred as just being the misprocessing of the Love.

Underneath hatred there is always Love, for we all are Love—that is our Life Instinct. Therefore, as long as we are alive we are Love.

I look back to their tortured faces and see their Love. Inside them, She is singing—always. Now to help them to hear!

Each of us is born with beauty within us which we desire to make manifest and share during our lifetime. What better way to achieve this fundamental human drive for creative expression than through the arts? All we need is permission. All we need is love.

—RICHARD A. LIPPIN, M.D.

Art, prayer and healing all come from the same source, the human soul and . . . the energy that fuels these processes is the basic force of life, the force of creativity and of love.

—RICHARD A. LIPPIN, M.D.,
on Michael Samuels, M.D.

ALTHOUGH I AM THE FOUNDER of the Institute for Music and Health, my real work is with neither music nor health.

I try to go beyond them. To the Spirit behind all music, and all creativity—and all life. To the Eternal Eros, to Love.

And to go beyond the usual understanding of health to the ultimate cure for all suffering, the only cure—to the Spirit, to Love.

The day will come when,
after harnessing the winds, the tides, and gravitation,
we shall harness for God the energies of love.
And on that day, for the second time in the history of the world,
man will have discovered fire.

— TEILHARD DE CHARDIN

Hatred which is completely vanquished by love, passes into love.

— SPINOZA

The deepest suffering
is not the inability
to realize our Perfection,
but the inability to manifest It.

Not the knowledge
that we are Love,
but the expression of It.

The deepest suffering
is Love imprisoned.
Eros bound.

I don't work just to help you
know you are Love,
but to help you act on It—to live It.

SEX PROBLEMS AREN'T

Sex problems never are
—they're heart troubles
manifested in the genitals.

Impotence is partial
enlightenment:
too loving
to make hate,
but not yet
enough
to make love.

THERAPEUTIC ZEAL

the zeal of my soul formed into wishes for . . . recovery.

— VERNEY

AS FAR BACK as I can remember I always wanted to be a doctor. I have always been possessed of therapeutic zeal, so I can't understand why everyone doesn't want to be a therapist of one type or another. Why become an accountant or a lawyer when you could be a doctor of medicine, chiropractor, osteopath, psychotherapist. The modality doesn't matter just as long as there is the opportunity to deliver therapeutic care.

I believe that we all have this therapeutic zeal, this passionate desire to heal. So if my reasoning is correct, every non-healing profession must have been undertaken as a perversion, as a denial, of this deep impulse within us. What is it? The desire to be therapeutic is an expression of the maternal drive which we all possess, for it is an aspect of the life drive, what Freud called the Eros, which impels us all.

As mentioned earlier, this was beautifully described, in part, by Bruno Bettelheim[45] as: "It was our love for others, and our concern for the future of those we love, that Freud had in mind when he spoke of 'eternal Eros,' the love for others—the working of eternal Eros—finds its expression in relations we form with those who are important to us and what we do to make a better life, a better world for them."

Certainly a caring accountant or a lawyer—and there are a few of them—is helping to make a better world for us, but this is such a minor manifestation of the "Eternal Eros."

Could it be that everyone wants to be therapeutic but few undertake it because of a particular inhibition? This is exactly what I find. For, at a deep level, we all have the desire to be therapeutic, and would be but for a specific negativity relating to the small intestine meridian, which has sadness as its negative attribute. Specifically it is Small Intestine 15: there are tears inside me that cannot come out. Frequently this relates to a loss early in life—strangely enough, often through the absence of an unknown relative. An example of this would be a grandmother whom you never knew, for she died before you were born—but your mother mourned for her and passed on this sadness to you.

I once was involved in a research project to find out why so many young nurses quit their training. I found that all of them had entered nursing because of a very strong desire to heal, often because these women had a close relative, usually the father, who was chronically ill and whom they hoped to, as it were, heal by nursing their patients. A time would come, usually quite early in their training, when they would become disillusioned, when their therapeutic hopes would be dashed. This was usually with the death of a patient with whom they had formed an attachment. As if to say, if he has died on me, so will my father—so what is the point of becoming a nurse? Then they would quit, the tears inside never released, their therapeutic zeal destroyed.

In some of them I was able to reactivate it, but not many—I wish I had known then what I know now, specifically about Small Intestine 15. For it is possible to reactivate this therapeutic zeal, which may seem dead but has only really been dormant—usually since early childhood. This does not mean that the retailer then closes up his shop and now becomes a psychotherapist, but rather that he sees himself more as ministering to the people with whom he comes into contact—whatever his occupation, caring for them, endeavoring to better their lives. Of course, this especially applies to his loved ones at home.

And most therapists also have some Small Intestine 15 sadness lurking inside them which, when it is released, greatly enhances their therapeutic powers.

To summarize: the desire to help others, to be therapeutic, is an expression of the maternal drive, an essential part of "Eternal Eros," the drive for life that is the very basis of our existence. Frequently this is specifically inhibited by a long-standing sadness and when this is overcome, our ability to give out our love is greatly increased. For this is the basis of all true therapy, which is, as Freud wrote, "in essence a cure through love."

Imprisonment is suffering
because it deprives us
of our ability
to act meaningfully.

And the greatest suffering
is the inability to act
on our strongest drive
—Eros,
the expression of Life,
of Love.

"BARBERRY BARK!"

WHILE BEING VISITED by a medical doctor, a chiropractor, two psychic healers, and a herbalist, I suffered an accident in which a finger became swollen and very painful. Over the next few hours they all tried to help me, each according to his own lights. But all without success.

That night, still in pain, I eventually fell into a fitful sleep. Suddenly I was awakened by a loud voice which I knew was in the right side of my head, but seemed somehow to be outside me—up, and to my right. It was a voice of utter authority and so powerful that it had to be male. It was as if God were speaking directly to me. Just two words, "Barberry bark!"

I went downstairs to my office and found a small container of it. I'd never used it before, could remember nothing about its properties, but I decided to take it. And it was "I" who decided. I did not feel compelled to, as if punishment would be inflicted on me if I didn't. It was not that I had been commanded to take it, but strongly advised.

And within a few moments of chewing a piece of the bark, the pain vanished!

When I awoke in the morning, the pain was still gone, but now "I" made a mistake. "I" decided to take some more—just to ensure that the pain did not recur. And just as quickly as the first had removed the pain, the second brought it back! I had acted without the advice of my Muse.

I believe that one of the greatest books of the last century is *The Origin of Consciousness in the Breakdown of the Bicameral Mind* by Julian Jaynes.[46] He states that until a few millennia ago, mankind was ruled (that is, human conduct controlled) by our inner voice, the Muse—a god who was automatically obeyed. And this voice spoke from the speech center in the right brain hemisphere, as mine had done.

As society became more complex, the Muse message for human conduct required increasingly more complex adaptations to the ever more complex realities of the external world. This led to what Jaynes called the breakdown of the bicameral mind and the consequent origin of the sense of self.

But the Muse is still always there. It is, I believe, the Creative Unconscious, the Eternal Eros.

And It, as it were, wanted to help me that night of my pain. So It gave me the answer—I had presumably stored in my unconscious the properties of the Barberry bark.

But unlike the man before the breakdown of the bicameral mind, I—my ego—had the choice to respond to, to obey, the Muse—or not. I chose to, with great benefit. But in the morning "I" went ahead without the Muse.

I have tried since then to be ever-mindful of the Muse. There is a god within each of us that knows—that is the Love, the Eternal Eros. It is not a quiet, still voice. It resonates with authority, if "we"—our egos—choose to listen.

We need our egos to survive, but survival will depend on the ego working in perfect harmony with the Muse, so as to best manifest Love into our troubled world.

THE TURBINE

WHEN AS A MEDICAL STUDENT I tried to study biochemistry, I became overwhelmed by the hundreds of equations and diagrams. They were so confusing because they seemed not to make broad sense. There seemed to be no overall perspective, just so many little independent facts.

I spent nearly a year preparing a large master flowchart showing all the biochemical reactions in our textbooks, all displayed out there before me in a way that made it so all-encompassingly logical. (And I was especially proud that on the whole chart with its myriad flow lines, not one line cut across another, so carefully had I laid them out.)

What gave it all sense was that in the center, in pride of place, was the citric acid cycle, the turbine of all biochemical reactions. Into it directly or, more commonly, indirectly, cascaded all the biochemical reactions. And it was fueled by oxygen.

Now it was all so clear. There is the citric acid cycle—and into it are flowing hundreds of lines of action, each along its own path. Everything in its place and everything feeding its energy into the giant central turbine. It all made sense!

And here I am nearly fifty years older, and trying now to make sense not just of biochemistry, but of human nature.

I have just visited a book superstore, buying from the following sections: philosophy, children's, self-help, medical, biology, linguistics, psychology, theology, eastern spirituality, reference, music, art, theater, poetry, the classics, literature, history, evolution, ethology, and anthropology! Trying to make sense of human nature! Of all the thousands of interactions, of the flowing and intermingling lines of human activity in so many of its manifestations.

And in my mind I can construct a chart like the one I made of biochemistry. I can see the interplays of philosophy and history and theology, of linguistics and psychology. And so on, and so on. And so on—to where?

In the center, where all the lines eventually converge, is a giant turbine—the Spiritual Life. Into it flow all the activities of every human being. Here is the very hub of human nature. And it is fueled by Love.

LOVE

Love is a stranger and speaks a strange language.

—RUMI

THAT IS OUR problem.

Here are the sayings of some who knew Her:

Love is a spirit all compact of fire,
Not gross to sink, but light, and will aspire.

—SHAKESPEARE

Love conquers all things: Let us too give in to Love.

—VIRGIL

Love is all we have, the only way
that each can help the other.

—EURIPIDES

Love alone
Is the true seed of every merit in you.

—DANTE

Love is a circle that doth restless move
In the same sweet eternity of love.

—ROBERT HERRICK

I have become the One I love, and he whom I love has become
myself! We are two spirits, mingled in one body! Thus, to see me
is to see him, and to see him is to see us.

—AL-HALLAJ

Nothing is sweeter than Love, nothing stronger, nothing higher,
nothing wider, nothing more pleasant, nothing fuller nor better
in Heaven and earth.

—THOMAS À KEMPIS

And most of all, in terms of healing:

Expansion is life.
Love is expansion.
Love is therefore
the only law of life.

—VIVEKANANDA

LOVE, THE VERB

Love is a transitive verb.
The most transitive of all,
for its object is everyone.

ALL NOUNS, FENOLLOSA declared, started life as verbs, as actions—only later becoming static, petrified into nouns.[47]

Thus, love the verb is greater than love the noun.

Therefore, I believe the greatest tragedy is not the not knowing of love—of feeling unloved—but in the not doing it—in not loving. For we all possess Eros, the drive to love, and to not love is to be inhibited, castrated.

The just-divorced man sits alone, lonely in his deserted room on a Saturday night. Too castrated to love. Too castrated to realize that you don't need to have a mate to love, that you can—No! You must—love everything, every one. All of Life—including your ex-wife. This is Eros unbound.

When we feel loved we want to love in return. And when we love we also feel loved. And want to love even more in return.

I have written a great deal about the baby's reciprocation of the mother's love—his love in response to hers. His Belovingness in response to the Belovedness he feels from her.

But we must remember that the baby, too, is endowed, imbued, blessed with Eros. He also has the drive to love her, as she has to love him. And, of course, the more love he feels from her, the more he is motivated to give his in response. And the mother, too.

Basic to all love the noun is love the verb—the drive, the impulse, the action.

So no matter what the circumstances, this drive needs to be always fully expressed. Love must out!

There is more than Perfection:
there is Perfection in action.
That is Love.

XII.
CREATIVITY

———❈———

CREATIVITY

my soul roams and soars through the universe
on the wings of imagination

—ROUSSEAU

I TRY TO DEDICATE myself increasingly to the relief of human suffering through the Arts. Not turning my back on all else I have learned in my years in medicine, in psychiatry, and in life, but using all of this to enhance Creativity—the highest choices for Art, and for Life. For as in one's art, so in one's life.

High Creativity is, at every moment, the best choice for love and for life. This, I believe, we can most readily achieve by practicing the Creative Arts, most of all Music.

The Perfection, the God or Goddess Within, the Muse, the Thusness, the Numinous, the Fountain of Life Energy or of Love—all are the same. All just metaphors for the Indescribable which is within us, which is Us.

It is my passionate belief that through music, True Music, we can most easily and most closely approach the Unknowable.

THE LITTLE THINGS

Photography teaches me
to see the little things,
not the wide river—
too much—much too much—
but the tiny ripples
flowing round the twig.

I learn to love Her
through Her tiny things.

ON THE DAY THE DIAGNOSIS was made, when my father knew he would die, he taught me what his older brother had passed on to him when he too confronted his mortality. I realize now, he said, that what matters in life is the little things. The little things—like a blade of grass.

For years I took innumerable photographs of the little things. And my favorite is of just the tip of a single blade of grass.

I sometimes spent hours in a stream capturing the flow of tiny eddies around the smallest pebbles. Never the whole stream, never a large rock. Too much. Just the tiny little movements, the little plays of life.

Trying with every exposure to understand my father's teaching. I came to learn that he was right—God is most manifest in the little things.

I try to pass on his wisdom, as it had been passed on to him, to my students. Encouraging them to look through their viewfinders, the images magnified, to find that special Numinous wonder, that particular Epiphany, that comes from beholding the All in the minute: Heaven in a grain of sand.

I learned to train my photographer's eye on the little things around me. Like now—the infinite plays of gold point and black shadow on white, as this nib dances across the page.

Especially I encourage you to look at the little things that make up the totality of your loved ones: the very corner of her mouth, the little striations on her lip, each eyelash.

Infinite tiny blessings. Every thing about her face is infinite—infinitely Beautiful, infinitely Beloving.

And then bring all these infinites together, amalgamate each intimation of her Self into the totality that is Her, revealed before you in all Her radiant glory.

I can always tell an artist or a photographer by the way their eyes move—constantly alighting on a new visual delight, inwardly recording it, then darting on to the next—like a ceaseless bee. Their minds filled with thousands upon thousands of little plays of forms, of shapes, and of colors. Each one unique and evanescent.

We all can be True Artists: every moment of our lives another glimpse of tiny boundless Delights. Getting to know so well the little things, we come to accept the Unknowable.

I cannot deal with a mountain,
let alone a vast panorama.
Too much, all too much.
Not even a little stream—
just a tiny eddy, no more.
A single leaf—or even less.
The smaller it is, the more I see God.

On the day he knew he would die
my father spoke as never before:
Now I know it's the little things that matter,
little things—like a blade of grass.

A LETTER TO A YOUNG SCULPTOR

The self is capable of apprehending something beyond the self.

—HERBERT READ,
"A Letter to a Young Painter"

DEAR CHRIS,

You know how much I admire your sculptures, and even more so your aspiration to make them as loving as possible, so that all who see them, touch them, or think on them, all who take them into their hearts, will come closer to a state of Belovedness. And by this, as by all Great Art, will their suffering be ameliorated.

Let me suggest a way by which you can come closer to achieving your aspiration. We will use as an example the bust of Christina that you are making at the moment.

As you well know, the essence of great sculpture is to go deep into your subject, deep into Christina, to her very heart's core. And then to go to the same place, deep to the very heart's core, of the model of her. The feeling of Beauty from each of these holy places should be identical, should be resonating in perfect tune with each other. To reassure yourself of this, place yourself first in Christina's Center and from there look outward, and feel outward, in all directions. Then do the same with her model. There should be more perfect harmony.

Every piece of clay that you add and every single sculpting movement should, of course, increase the physical likeness, but also must always maintain the spiritual unity. Always sculpt from that Center, never from the skin.

And when you have finished, you will have given the world a sculpture of Christina—and More: an external representation of the inner Beauty, the Perfection, that is her. It was This that you saw and felt in your heart's core, and it was This that you have now made manifest to the world. So all who gaze on her may see through her their own Perfection, for this is the purpose of Art, the deepest reason for its existence.

But, you ask, where is her heart's core? Is there any such point? I believe there is, and it is not one of those commonly taught in meditation, for example the *hara*. I refer to it as the Inner Temple, and I have found that concentrating on this point, meditating on it, being constantly aware of it, will raise the Life Energy more than any other. It appears to so center a person that it could be called the psychic center.

To find it, run your finger backward from the lower border of your ear. As your finger comes backward let it outline the rounded lower bulge of the mastoid process of the temporal bone, and then let your finger trace this outline upward as it continues back until it stops in a small depression, which is on about the same horizontal line as the opening to the ear. Anatomically this is called the digastric fossa.

Place the finger of one hand on one fossa and that of another hand on the other. Now point your fingertips at each other and then point them forward just a little bit. Then imagine their meeting point inside your skull. This is the Inner Temple which I have found after many years of clinical exploration. I encourage my students to concentrate on this Temple, to try to be constantly aware of it.

I call it a temple because I suggest they place in it their most sacred objects, their icons. In mine there are a number, especially one of my wife Susan's special smile; and some of my mother—when we made daisy chains for each other; when she gave me a puppy for a birthday present and he ran back and forth between the two of us as a messenger of our love; when she held Susan's hand and mine in hers and gazed so deeply into our eyes; and last, the sacred image of her body just after the moment of her death. It is indeed for me a holy place.

I have found that if I place my fingers on a sufferer's digastric fossae and imagine them meeting at his Inner Temple, he will be almost immediately greatly relieved. And in terms of your work, I have found that I can bring about this change by just looking at the sufferer, by looking deep into him, into his Inner Temple. It is as if this actuates his own awareness of his Beauty, his Belovedness. This would appear to be a most powerful Life Energy-enhancing procedure.

You can do this every moment you are sculpting: every moment you can concentrate on Christina's Inner Temple, on her limitless inner Beauty. And this will be made manifest into the world in its replication in clay. Furthermore, your recognition of her Inner Temple will cause her to radiate even more of the Love within her, even more for you to replicate.

It has been said by an art critic, and I believe it is unfortunately true, that no work of art has ever relieved human suffering. Perhaps yours will be the first.

THE REASON FOR ART

The spirit, in its artistic striving for reunion with nature,
is the art-work.

— WAGNER

I HAVE SPENT MANY thousands of hours researching and examining thousands upon thousands of musical performances, dances, paintings, photographs, sculptures, poems, and books. There is so much about the Life Energy to be learned in all these acts of creation. And I have used this knowledge time and time again to help people play Bach better, and Beethoven, and Arlen, and Gershwin, and Rodgers and Hart.

But that is never what I have really wanted to do. I have wanted to learn all that so as to distill it down to its pure essence, to a simple single song that can be delivered to a sufferer, anywhere in the world, in any situation, regardless of language. Delivered in such a way that his suffering is overcome.

That is all that matters in all of art, for that is the reason for its existence. And that should be all that matters in us, for that is the reason for our existence.

CREATIVITY AND ENTHUSIASM

Nothing great was ever achieved without enthusiasm.

— EMERSON

THERE ARE MANY everyday expressions that show an unconscious relationship between giving birth to a baby and giving birth to an idea, both of them being acts of creativity. For example, we speak of someone having a fertile imagination, as being a fertile source of new ideas. We use the word *pregnant* to refer to a profusion of ideas, teeming with ideas. Fertile, imaginative, inventive. We speak of *seminal* in relationship to having the power to originate ideas, to be creative. We speak of the birth of an idea, and of Beethoven laboring to give birth to a symphony.

It is interesting that from the Indo-European root *gen*, to give birth, to beget, are derived such words as *generate* (including the generation of ideas), *genius* (one full of ideas), *germ* (of an idea), and *pregnant* itself. We also speak of conceiving an idea, and of concepts.

For our acts of creativity to be truly Creative, that is, therapeutic, they must arise out of a deep desire to conceive them, to generate them, to incubate them, and then to deliver them into the world. This generative impulse must be as strong, as overriding, as the maternal instinct, of which it is, in its own way, a particular example.

But if there is an inhibition of this deep desire to give birth to the products of our creativity, then there will be no real therapy. This is what I find so often to be the case: the sufferer does not want to beget and give birth to his creativity, to the songs from his Creativity.

This comes about as a result of a particular problem concerning the thyroid meridian, whose negative attribute is that of depression. Specifically it relates to Thyroid 1, the enthusiasm problem. When the sufferer is imbued with enthusiasm, his creativity is high. He is fecund and fertile. But when his enthusiasm is low, he at best just goes through the motions of being creative, with little effect—it is but a pseudo-pregnancy, and any labor is only false.

Enthusiasm is defined as "intensity of feeling in favor of a person, principle, cause, etc.; passionate eagerness in any pursuit." Another definition for us is "poetical fervor." It is derived from *en*, in, and *theos*, God—hence inspired, filled with spirit. And it is this spirit that, as it were, inseminates the creator, that drives him passionately to deliver his products of creativity, his babies, into the world—all as manifestations of the spirit by which he feels possessed.

Without this spirit, this enthusiasm, there can be no "poetical fervor," no acts of high Creativity, no true healing.

It is of little value to sing or dance or meditate or to carry out any other spiritual endeavor if the spirit is not in it, for then it is not really a spiritual endeavor at all.

It is for this reason that it is critically important to assess whether the sufferer has enthusiasm—can enthusiastically embrace the therapy, whatever it may be. If it is not there, if it has been inhibited, then he must correct the specific trauma that caused him to make the choice against enthusiasm, against being inspired, against being filled with spirit.

And let us not forget that the therapist himself must be filled with enthusiasm—overflowing with it. He must be possessed by "poetical fervor."

THERAPEUTIC WRITING

EVERYONE HAS A PURPOSE for writing. And so, of course, have I. But it is not really to give you information. This is only a secondary purpose. The main one is to raise your Life Energy. I have tried to make my writings themselves as therapeutic as possible. This has been my intention, and I have examined and tested them all in an endeavor to ensure this.

My hope is that as you continue to read in the right frame of mind, in the right frame of heart, your Life Energy may be enhanced. This, I believe, must be the primary reason for all communication.

The first criterion for therapeutic writing is that the writer must have this intention—the desire and the drive to help alleviate inner suffering through his writing. But however well intended, however well written, however expertly expressed, its therapeutic effect will be minimal unless the second criterion is also satisfied.

And this is that the writing itself be therapeutic—not the message, but the medium. Not the material or the form in which it is presented, but the flow, the rhythm. No, not exactly that. More so, the pulse form of its movement. How close is it to the inner pulse of the writer, how close to The Pulse?

That is to say, how much of his ego has been placed at the service of the Muse? How close is the content, the meaning, to being at one with the Spirit, the true Self of the writer? Does his writing move—does he move—as It moves?

To put it another way, how much Life Energy, how much Healing Power, is in the communication? For this is what matters most.

The first criterion gives us only facts, and, however well intended, will only bring about an inner change in those readers about to change anyway. It, as it were, flips over those already on the cusp.

But when there is high Life Energy in the message as well as information, then the base of the cusp is greatly expanded and many more sufferers will cross over. For now that their Life Energy has been actuated, they want to embrace health and life. Now they are reading not just with their brains, but also with their hearts. And all great inner changes originate in the heart.

It's not so much the lyrics—it's the singing.

To be truly therapeutic, the writer must always speak from his heart, never just from his brain, for only from the heart will it go to the heart.

A NEW DEFINITION OF PSYCHOSIS

All that we are is the result of what we have thought.

— DHAMMAPADA

PSYCHOSIS IS USUALLY defined as a severely impaired capacity to deal with reality. The word *psyche*, which is Greek in origin, translates as *spirit* or *soul*. So psychosis, according to this idea, is an impairment of the soul, a soul disease. The Indo-European root is *bhes*, pronounced "bess," which means "to breathe," and it is said to be alliterative, in other words it is an imitation of the sound of breathing. So breath, soul, spirit, psyche, psychosis are all related.

In the usual meaning of the word, a man is psychotic because "he cannot handle things in the outside world." I would suggest a change in the definition of psychosis, so that, rather than considering external reality, it is instead seen predominantly as an impairment of the handling of inner reality. And the most basic inner Reality is that we all are Perfect, that we all are Spiritual Beings, that we all have psyches, souls—in a sense, we all *are* psyches. So I would define psychosis as the loss of this center. Even if we once did, we now no longer believe that at our central core we are Perfect, we are Gods, Buddhas, or whatever metaphor you want to use.

If you do not have that core knowledge, you are always wandering blindly through life without a central focus, without a central hub around which everything revolves. To me, a psychotic is someone who is like King Lear wandering through the wilderness—blind, lost, aimless. Never mind the external reality, it is the internal reality that really matters. That is what Lear lost—the internal reality.

What stops us gaining this core knowledge is the belief that we are so bad that we do not even want to look inside for it. For this, there must be what I call the courage to have insight. You have to have an inkling that even if there is dross on the surface, when you dive under it everything is going to be all right—you are going to find the Perfection. That takes courage and trust. And most people suffer because they lack this courage. Somehow they have lost the belief that deep down inside them is a wonderful Center. Being cut off from that makes them, by my definition, psychotic.

So what do we have? We have people who say, "My life is suffering, please help me." We have other people who say, "My life is suffering—but he did it," which is without insight, or, the most common response, "There's nothing much wrong with me." Remember Walter Mitty: "It's nothing—just a broken arm!"

So as treaters or therapists, we constantly have a battle in which we have to fight both the sufferers and their illnesses. We are almost forced to try to impose our will to be well onto them, because they will not allow us to help them actuate their own will. This is always a fight. They do not keep appointments, they do not come back, they argue—and all because there is no student-teacher relationship. They are desperately frightened to look inside. So when you find someone who is psychotic, it is because they have lost contact with their Center, because they will not look inside. And how do you help them to overcome this?

One of the best ways is by coming around the problem with Music. Encourage the student to look inside the music, look inside the composer, then look inside other people (especially his mother), and, finally, look inside himself. Often it works; sometimes it does not. It just depends on how skillful you are and how much the student hates himself, how psychotic he is. If he will not let you do that, there is not much you can do, apart from waiting until, like Lear, he cries out in pain from the wilderness. And then all you can do is stop the pain. You still cannot get him to his Center.

So many people go through life never finding out how wonderful they are. They spend all their lives in a state of psychosis. This is the greatest tragedy. I hope through the work with Creativity we may be able, one day, to overcome some of it.

He who has found Spirit, is Spirit.

—Mundaka Upanishad

"Every June I go off, and then
every October I come good again.
What makes me go wrong in June?"

"What makes you come right in October?"

"Ah! That's a *good* question!"

Whether you
marry—or not,
divorce—or not,
even live—or not,
is not
my real concern.

Only to help you
raise your Life Energy
for you to then make
the Creative choices
for you
in your existence.

XIII.
THE MOTHER

❦

When she takes her true place before the altar of the infinite
she casts off her dark veil and bares her face to the beholder
as a revelation of supreme joy.

—TAGORE

MY CREDO

THIS I BELIEVE:

Earth, as concomitant of its apparent existence, is at this time inhabited by some species (so we name them) who have the particular attribute of what we call love. They have the consciousness to recognize it and the ability to choose to use it.

This capacity, this quirk of Existence, appears to be most highly endowed in those that men call Mankind, and it is an essential component of the breeding process, increasing the likelihood of human survival: the more the mother and father love their child, the greater its chances of reaching maturity and itself breeding another generation.

And for its offspring to mature, it must also have the capacity to love its child. And this it "learned" when it was itself a child.

The parents love their child, and it responds with love to them, and then later to its own children. So on and on—for the period of human existence.

The awareness of this love appears to be a particular characteristic of human existence. It seems to us to come from our mother (and later, our father). From her we learn of love: to feel it, to know it—and then to return it. She teaches the lesson of love.

She is to her child the creator of love, and heaven is in her arms. But this Feeling fades, is even forgotten—and at risk is human survival. Another quirk of our existence is, as it were, called into action to prevent this: we become attracted to certain colors, shapes and sounds, configurations of Existence. These remind us of the early love and thus encourage us to love. The tree becomes holy when it reminds us of her.

We need—we must find—her love. Have it reaffirmed. We seek it in Nature, in art, in the sky, and in our concept of God. And also in our spouses—for if the parents cannot find their mothers' love in each other, they will not find it in their child.

But, basically, we must seek her, find her, in herself—and she in her mother and her child.

And here, I believe, is the very nub of our existence in this Existence: the mother finding her own mother's love in the child that she is bearing.

You have only to aspire to keep yourself open to the Mother . . .
and to let her work in you.

—SRI AUROBINDO

Stop. Be still.
Strain to hear
the Song of your Muse,
and go to Her,
to your Home.

HEAVEN ON EARTH

let
Blue skies be your coverlet.

—LORENZ HART

THE WORD *heaven* comes from the root *kam*, "to cover," from which is also derived such words as *camisole* and *chemise*.

And the Great Comforter was, and is, the mother.

Comfort ye,
Comfort ye, my darling,
saith your Mom.

The voice of him
that crieth
in the wilderness
was me
in my cot.
And always
she came
and comforted.

To sleep is to return into the womb of the mother. And it is surprising how difficult it is to sleep when we are uncovered. We need to, as it were, feel her arms around us, protecting and comforting. We need this reassurance. To fall asleep within her, covered by her amnion. No wonder a coverlet, especially one for a baby, is called a comforter (as is a dummy teat put into the baby's mouth to quieten it).

So heaven is to feel covered and comforted. Heaven is the mother at her most loving. When we know her as This, then and only then will we at last find Heaven on Earth.

Heaven is not another place but the total understanding
and acceptance of the present reality.

—FRANCIS COOK

Thou art one with her, and knowest not of self
in thy supreme joy.

—Blake

All troubles pass
when the mother
is seen as Divine.

ON EROS

Love is the union of spirits. Love is spiritual fire, spiritual heat.

— SWEDENBORG

To FREUD, EROS WAS much more than sexual love, it was the very drive for life.

What is Eros for me?

In Hesiod's *Theogeny*, Eros was "a primeval God, son of Chaos, the original primeval emptiness of the Universe." Thus it is Eros who gives sense to our existence. The *Encyclopaedia Britannica* continues, "to Hesiod, Eros was the fertilizing force that united Heaven and Earth."

We look up to heaven, always above us, lovingly smiling down, as the baby looks up to his mother. And in her arms, comforted by her love, we have found Heaven. Heaven is Belovedness by the mother.

And Earth is me below, beloved by the bestower of Belovedness and filled with Belovingness for her.

It is her love and mine in reciprocation that unite us, that enable each of us to find Heaven and Earth. It is her Eros, and hers as mine, that produces my world, my Heaven on Earth.

The one word "filial" is the gateway to all mysteries.

—TSUNG-TSE

THE FIRST FULL BREATH OF LIFE

And the breath divine is love.

—BLAKE

THERE ARE MOMENTS in Nature, in Music, in Marriage, when we are reminded of the Heaven we knew, at times, in the Womb.

It is for this that we gaze at sunsets, listen to Bach—and fall in love. For birth is the expulsion from Eden, never to be reentered except by those few who find Heaven, everywhere and always, on Earth.

The rest of us can only lift our eyes to the sky and hope for Heaven in an afterlife—like the Heaven we had in our prelife, in the Maternal Land of Belovedness.

The process of birth should not have been a trauma, just a peaceful transmigration from one state to another, from one Heaven to another.

And we, now, in this world, will only find Heaven again when the physical distortions impressed on us in our troubled passage through the birth canal are at last corrected. For it is this lifelong affliction that has forever prevented us from knowing the Peace and Belovedness of this existence.

Only when we take, at last, the first full breath of life denied us at birth will our bodies finally expand—and our eyes be opened to the Belovedness all around.

There was a continual perception of Sanctity
in the whole of nature.

—RUSKIN

TRUE HOLISTIC HEALING

Each soul is potentially divine. The goal is to manifest
this divine within.

—VIVEKANANDA

LET US START WITH DOGEN'S teaching that we all are always Perfect, and that our central problem in life is that we do not realize it and we therefore live our lives accordingly. All of our higher endeavors to overcome the suffering will be successful only when we embrace the heart knowledge of our innate Goodness, our innate Godliness.

It is my belief that we can only realize This about ourselves when we are in the state of Belovedness, when we feel loved, totally, ever-constantly, by another. By the Other. By our own mothers, our creators, nurturers, and protectors—our first "God."

Only a Sage knows his mother's Perfection, and therefore his own. The rest of us live out our existence as lives of suffering, ever unenlightened.

Strange as it may seem, if I twist your head and neck into a particular distorted position, in that position alone you will suddenly come closer to a feeling of love—the love that is within you. This "love within" can be called by many metaphors, the Muse, the Wellspring of Creativity, Freud's Eternal Eros, the Drive for Life, the Buddha nature, and so forth.

There is within us a kernel of Perfect Wisdom, a Muse. If we but listened to Its Song and used our ego skills to adapt this internal message for health and love and life to our present realities—both internal and external—then and only then would we be at peace. For only then would we ever be truly cured of our suffering. I refer to this distortion of the Song as the ego-misprocessing of the Muse message. The Muse can be considered the ultimate homeostatic agent within us, constantly attempting to rebalance our Life Energy to keep us in harmony, in health.

Every negative wish and thought and action comes from this ego-misprocessing, otherwise we would lead lives of high Life Energy—living the life of the Song of the Muse, adapted to the present-day realities. Completely in tune with the soul within and the world without.

All negativity, all illness, all evil, is just ego-misprocessing of this Drive for Life, our greatest possession.

Why is it that if I twist your head and neck into a particular extremely distorted position, suddenly a point will be found where you are devoid, cleansed, as it were, of most of these negativities? It goes back, as all our problems do, to the womb—and then to the birth process. Let us first consider the womb.

No mother totally loves her baby, for no mother feels, or felt, totally loved by her mother. And her baby equals her mother. So any negativity she felt from her mother, which she has not yet resolved, will be passed on to her baby. This negativity the baby will feel, for he lives in a sea of feelings. He will hear it in her voice. And he will sense it in the disturbed patterns of her respiration, in which he is rocked or tossed, depending on the inconstancies of her love.

I believe that it is from the loving mother's respiratory movements imposed on the baby in the womb that all music, and hence all art, originates.

What is the baby's defense against this negativity that he feels all around him? I believe that he distorts his body, especially his head, trying to turn away from the negativity. It is the only defense a helpless creature has. This first twist from the normally healthy body attitude is probably the start of the ego-misprocessing. It imposes, if I am correct, a vestibulo-cerebellar problem, which I believe is basic to all human suffering.

This body distortion is exacerbated a thousand-fold by the birth process, by the horror of this supreme trauma. I often wonder whether the fear of death is that, deep down, we believe it will be as fearful as our birth.

From this very moment of birth, if we examine it correctly, as the cranial osteopaths do, we will find that the baby's body is greatly distorted. If it is not corrected he will be doomed from birth to a life of suffering. We must also remember that the more distortion the mother received from her mother, the more distorted will be her own baby's pregnancy and birth. And the more distorted she is, the more she will misprocess her maternal instinct, compounding still further the distortions of birth.

It is this that I was trying to demonstrate above, showing that for every person there is one particular body distortion which, strange as it may seem, bizarre as it may look, actually in a sense corrects the birth distortion. So to walk through life in this twisted way would produce less misprocessing of the Drive for Life than maintaining our bodies in our apparently "normal" attitude, which is itself really but another distortion imposed on top of the initial one.

What does it all come down to? I believe that, in one sense, our life problems are spiritual. In particular, that we are alienated, estranged from our mothers who, each in her own distorted and incomplete way, tried to love us according to the impulse of love which is the maternal instinct. We spend our lives never really feeling the love that she so wanted to give us, but could give only imperfectly because of her own misprocessing problems. We yearn for her Love, we yearn to live in a state of Belovedness—and we suffer because we believe that we are not there. But we are. We always are. We just have to sense what she wanted to do: her Muse, her Maternal Instinct.

So all of our problems are spiritual—and yet they are all physical too. Because the more we work with the physical body to overcome the distortions, as does a skilled cranial osteopath, for example the late Dr. Robert Fulford or Dr. Edgar Miller, the more the vestibulo-cerebellar imbalance is corrected. Thus the more the crippling intrauterine and birth distortions are overcome, the more spiritual we become, for the more we see our mothers as Love, and the more we then so see ourselves.

Just physically correcting as far as possible the birth (and pre-birth) distortions is not enough, for the problem is also a spiritual one. So the healer must deal with both the physical and the spiritual imbalances simultaneously. He must constantly be aware of the soul of the sufferer whose head he holds in his hands. And to welcome this most intimate and holy union, and reverence it, humbly. It is work on the body, but always with the Highest Purpose.

Thus, the mundane, the work with the physical body, can lead us to the supramundane, the Spirit. And the Spirit requires the mundane in order to be manifest. Mundane and supramundane, intertwined, united as one. This is true holistic healing.

Many practitioners talk of the "body-mind-spirit" triangle. If we must pursue this artificial categorization, then the odd one out, the unnecessary one, is the mind. This is the dead end. To pursue this will lead us nowhere. Freud knew this, which is why he spoke of the soul. Psychoanalysis for him was the analysis of psyche, the soul.

What we might call psychological problems are really the consequence of distortions of the body, as I have pointed out above, or else minor manifestations of the eternal spiritual problem, the absence of Belovedness.

If we enter the no-man's land of psychotherapy we will never emerge cured, for the two essentials will never take place—the overcoming of the physical distortions since the beginning of life, and the feeling of Belovedness, of Spirit, also denied us since our very beginning.

So working just at the spiritual level will ultimately never be enough, nor will working just at the physical level. Both are needed working together, simultaneously. To me, this, and nothing less, is true holistic healing.

Some are born to sweet delight,
Some are born to endless night.

—BLAKE

It all primarily depends on feeling Beloved—or not.

And this primarily depends on how traumatic was the birth, and how much of the trauma was corrected.

> We never can feel
> truly loved
> by our mothers
> until we have overcome
> the trauma she inflicted
> at birth.

LIFE AFTER BIRTH

When the foolishness of the body will be cleared away and we shall be pure and hold converse with other pure souls, and know of ourselves the clear light everywhere; and this is surely the light of truth.

—PLATO

PLATO WAS REFERRING to life after death.

But I believe that we can "know of ourselves the clear light everywhere" when we at last overcome the lifelong uncorrected physical traumas inflicted at birth. This is the initial "foolishness of the body."

Then we may find at last life, real Life, after birth.

BIRTHING TRAUMA
AND ENLIGHTENMENT

OUR DEEPEST SUFFERING is our despair at the perceived impossibility of bringing together who we know we should be ("good") and who we believe we are ("bad").

To relieve our suffering, all we need do is to change our belief, to overcome the self-delusion of our "evil" by correcting the ego-misprocessing that prevents us realizing we are always Perfect.

All true Wisdom, all Knowledge, is this Enlightenment. Only with This will we ever be at Peace.

As just mentioned, misprocessing is basically a vestibulo-cerebellar dysfunction, strange as this may seem, having apparently to do with the body rather than the spirit.[48] It starts in the womb and is exacerbated a thousandfold by the uncorrected traumas of our births—and then aggravated by all subsequent traumas.

The ultimate answer for human suffering will be to bring into the world children who will never not be enlightened. This will come when Mothering is revered as the highest spiritual endeavor.

Think of loving and being loved;
I swear to you, whoever you are, you can interfuse
yourself with such things that everybody that sees
you shall look longingly upon you.

Think of spiritual results,
Sure as the earth swims through the heavens, does every
one of its objects pass into spiritual results.

— WHITMAN

And, for us,
these will only come to be
when the traumas of birth,
physical, then spiritual,
are finally overcome.

A HEALER AND HATRED

I recognize
Only one relationship: devotion

—TULSIDAS

EVERY DAY IN MY WORK I am forced to confront hatred: mothers hating their children, children hating their mothers; husbands hating wives, wives hating husbands—and on and on. And it was much worse back in my psychiatry days!

If he doesn't love her, then he hates her. These are the two polarities. There is no unlove, no neutral, grey middle ground. He either loves her or hates her, wants to embrace her or hurt her.

Why must there be hatred? Why not always only love? There have been many attempts to answer this most basic of all questions—here is just another.

We have been given the power to hate, to kill. It has always been in our genes: it has always been there as a necessity for the survival of our species. Without it, we would have perished millions of years ago.

Hatred is essential for us to defend ourselves in a life-threatening situation. Kill or be killed.

Yes, you agree, but what has that to do with a man hating his wife?

Well, suppose that, at the moment of hatred, he perceives her as threatening his life, as turning into a rampant tiger. Now his hatred is explicable, justified.

But in actuality she is not threatening his life, is not a tiger. His hatred has arisen out of his misperception of the reality.

And that is all hatred is—the inappropriate response, the inappropriate invocation of our survival instinct. Wanting to kill, even killing, when not life-threatened. He only thinks his life is threatened. That is his misperception, what I call his misprocessing of reality.

Paradoxically, and tragically, this misprocessing can frequently be so extreme that an expression of love can be interpreted as one of hate—with the consequent (in)appropriate response.

How many times did I see this in the mental hospital. How many times have I seen it in life—and, of course, in my practice.

One example from thousands: a husband and wife are at a pool party. He is standing in the water as she swims by. He admires her buttocks in action—is fascinated, excited, aroused. So he pats her bottom affectionately. She immediately stops swimming, stands up—and punches him in the face.

His gesture of love was misprocessed as hate—and her response was appropriate. She was defending herself as if under attack.

This inappropriate hatred starts where misprocessing starts. Mainly, as I have previously outlined, from the uncorrected body distortions caused by the trauma of the birth process, especially the distortion of the head and neck.

A man may be in a state of hatred toward his wife, hurling invectives at her. But if I correct (somewhat) the birth distortion, tilting his head just so, he instantly reverts to love. His hatred only arose out of his body distortion, present from birth. And so does his wife's hatred of him. Twisted bodies—twisted minds.

So, the misprocessing arises from the head being turned around at birth. And hatred is its consequence.

Hatred is just love turned around.

Hatred is *Eros* reversed.

Hatred is only *Sore*.

The more I remember this, the less judgmental I become. I don't take hatred seriously anymore. For I know it can be turned around into love.

> He doesn't hate her—
> he's only Sore.

GOD IS ME AND MY MOTHER

My mother's love always haunted me.

—GANDHI

I USE THE WORD *God* quite frequently in my writings, for it possesses such emotive power. But I leave you to interpret it according to your own lights.

For me, God has nothing to do with any religious belief. It is the Feeling of utter Belovedness I have known, at times, starting with my mother.

God is me
and my mother
making daisy chains
for one another.

And Love, for me, is That which I felt from her, and later from others, and which I try, at times, to reciprocate.

God is the perfection that we must aspire to realize.

—THE MOTHER

WHAT RELIGION ARE YOU?

I am a devout musician.

—CHARLIE PARKER

THE PSYCHOANALYST WANTS the analysand to know as little about him as possible, so as to encourage his fantasies. The holistic therapist does the opposite—he voluntarily brings the whole of himself to the therapeutic situation. For he believes that the better the sufferer knows him, the better he will know himself. And "Know thyself" is the holistic therapist's motto.

So, I am often asked about my religion:
Are you Buddhist, Taoist, Christian, Jew—or what?
Are you theist—or atheist?
Do you believe in God?
What God?
I am all of the above, and more
—and more.

I am a deist. I believe in, and reverence, the loving creative power of my parents, especially my mother's Maternal Instinct. And I feel no need, now, to venture from Home.

My religion is my mother and me.

I know of no other Christianity—
And of no other Gospel
Than the liberty, both of body and mind,
To exercise the Divine Arts of Imagination.

—BLAKE

The only God
to worship
is the human soul
in the human body.

—VIVEKANANDA

GOD AND MOTHER

In loving their mother, they loved not her body
but the thing that moved her body.

—CHUANG TZU

WHEN EINSTEIN SPOKE of God I do not believe that he meant "a being conceived as the perfect, omnipotent, omniscient originator and ruler of the universe, the principal object of faith and worship in monotheistic religions." I believe he was instead referring to the feeling of awe, of amazement, and of trust at the limitless, ultimately unknowable, yet obviously utterly logical, Existence of everything, as we as humans perceive it. He gloried and reveled and exalted in the wonders of this Existence.

He was undoubtedly an atheist, and an adeist, for God to him was not "a being of supernatural powers," it was the state of Existence.

In this sense, I, too, am an atheist and an adeist. But unlike Einstein and Freud, for example, I do believe that there is a feeling of God within each of us. By God I am referring to what Rudolf Otto called the Holy.[49] And more, what he called the Numinous, "this 'extra' in the meaning of 'holy' above and beyond the meaning of goodness."

It is my belief that this is the feeling of Belovedness, of being totally, purely, ever constantly Loved. Such as a baby feels, although inconstantly, streaming from his mother. It is this feeling, ephemeral as it was, that we seek again throughout our lives. It is for this that we raise our eyes toward heaven and supplicate. But we do not find it there, for it came not from up in the sky but from the souls of our mothers gazing down on us.

But the love was never perfect. In fact, tragically, it was nearly always distorted, perverted, turned from its natural direction—at times even reversed.

And yet we all know in our hearts that there is More to her than she was ever able to reveal. We yearn ever more for her sweet touches of the Holy that at times came through directly from her soul.

The cure for human suffering will come not from the sky, from some immaterial concept that we have imagined in desperation, but from the material goddess (and *material* comes from the same etymological root as *mother, mater*).

Look into your mother's eyes: go deep inside, deeper than her heart—deep, deep into her soul. There you will find the purest, purest Love, the Maternal Instinct ever yearning to be fully expressed, to be given totally, purely, selflessly, to you.

Worship the Mother that is, and was, and always will be your god, your mother. Live in the state of Belovedness. Dedicate to It your life in gratitude.

Look into the eyes of everyone around you, and into your own. See through all of them the deep, deep instinct to Love, the Soul that we all possess.

DIAMOND "THE RECLUSE"?

I loved, and was beloved again.

—BYRON

THEOPHAN WAS A HOLY Eastern Orthodox priest who lived a life of meditative isolation. Hence he became known as Theophan the Recluse.

To all the sufferers who wrote petitioning help, his advice was always the same: stand reverently before God with your mind in your heart and recite the Jesus Prayer. Always the same advice, for so strongly did he believe in it as being the basic solution to all human suffering.

What would I advise those writing to me in despair? What, to me, is the basic solution to all human suffering?

Stand reverently before your holiest image of your mother. Go deep inside her and find her Perfect Love, the Mother she so desired to Be. Realize that this Maternal Instinct is the same Eternal Eros, the drive for Love, that you, too, possess—as does everyone. You are Perfect, we all are Perfect. We all are Love, for we all live in the Land of Belovedness.

I pray that I may know in my very heart's core that I always live in the Land of Belovedness.

So prays Diamond, who wishes he were as single-minded in his prayer as Theophan.

BELOVEDNESS

We can only love when we already feel loved.
Belovedness precedes Belovingness.
Hence, it is more basic to affirm
my mother's love of me,
than my love of her.
And God loves me, rather than I love God.[50]

God is Love.

—1 JOHN 4:16

And everywhere is God. Everywhere Love.
The clouds, the trees, all life, all humanity.
Each its Thusness.
Each its own expression of Being.
Each its own Perfection, Beauty and Love.

Everywhere the Love!
I live in Love! I am Beloved!
I live in the Land of Belovedness!

BABY AND MOTHER,
MUSIC AND BELOVEDNESS

The lap of Comfort, the hands of God,
the home of the Lullaby.

A WOMAN I KNOW at last asks me if I can help her with her four-year-old daughter, who is obviously quite disturbed. For example, she will come into the room and, without even acknowledging our existence, sit there in the middle of the floor with a blanket over her head. Or else she will stay outside in the hallway, poking her tongue out at us through the glass door.

Now it is easy to blame the mother, to see her as using her daughter as a weapon against her ex-husband. But that's not the way to go. Nor do we want to label her daughter as a psychiatric case—in fact it's not even important that I see her at all.

Nor should my primary approach be to help the mother love her daughter—of course she wants to. Then what is stopping her?

The answer is always the same, the mother—in this case, the mother's mother. For we have the formula: baby = mother's mother.

The answer for the little girl is for me to help her mother to feel the love of her own mother. Then, having first felt the love of her mother, she will feel the love of her little girl, who will respond in kind. The answer is always to feel the Belovedness, and this must always start with feeling it from the mother's mother. This is the essence for helping all disturbed children.

And the easiest way to initiate the state of Belovedness is through music—not just music for entertainment but music for Belovedness, True Music. Then to sing It to the little girl and have her sing it back to her mommy.

The womb
is the Land
of Belovedness,
for both.
Into there
the mother
bestows her Love,
and from there
her baby's to her.

All day
I am the mother,
my office my womb.
And at night,
the child again,
my bed her womb.

I CAN OPENLY SPEAK of Love in the therapeutic situation, for it has nothing to do with the therapist personally, or with the sufferer.

All the Love is mother-surrogate.

To the healer, the sufferer is his mother to whom he gratefully returns her Love.

And to the sufferer, the healer is his mother from whom he receives Love and to whom he now gives It back in grateful return.

The healer must love the sufferer as his mother and be loved in return by the sufferer as his mother. For the ultimate healing is knowing the Love of one's own mother. This is the state of Belovedness, this is the Pure Land, this is Heaven on Earth.

However, only when the surrogate role is kept firmly in mind can the Love be true, be altruistic.

THE STAGES OF HEALING

1. The healer first opens his heart to feel his mother's Belovedness.

2. Then, open-hearted, he radiates this Love to the sufferer who opens his heart to receive the Belovedness, as if from his mother.

3. This Love he then returns to the healer whose heart is open to receive It, as if from his mother.

4. Finally, the sufferer himself becomes a healer.

XIV.
ASPIRATION, MUSIC,
AND THE PULSE

ASPIRATION

The tear that glisten'd in his eye
Drown'd not his purpose fix'd on high.

—SCOTT

There are two powers that alone can effect in their conjunction
the great and difficult thing which is the aim of our endeavor, a
fixed and unfailing aspiration that calls from below and a supreme
Grace from above that answers.

—SRI AUROBINDO

BEETHOVEN'S NINTH SYMPHONY and his *Missa Solemnis* were composed at virtually the same time, the opus numbers being respectively 123 and 125. And each of them is scored for the same instrumentation, the same chorus, and the same four soloists. Yet in one way they are profoundly different, and Beethoven himself knew this, for he dedicated the Mass, "From the heart, may it go to the heart."

Many times I have come across this same difference when recording a musician playing the same work, regardless of its nature, in a church

271

in contrast to a concert hall. He looks around him and becomes inspired by this extra dimension that he then infuses into his music. (Unfortunately this only occurs with the amateur, for the professional is too jaded—a gig is just another gig.)

This extra dimension I call Aspiration. It is the something more that Beethoven put into his Mass, that the amateur puts into his playing in church, and that we can put into every activity throughout our lives.

To refer to it as "something" more is to belittle the state of Aspiration. It is not a thing; to reify it is to demean it.[51] Rather, it is just the More. It is the extra dimension. The violinist with Aspiration is doing More than just playing. But what it is he doesn't know. It is just that there is more to what he is doing than what he is actually doing. For his music-making has a Higher Purpose. And so, we hope, has his life.

But what is the higher purpose? What is the goal? These are the wrong questions, for again they reify Aspiration, they bring it down to earth, and aspiration is a breathing up (*a,* "up," *spiro,*[52] "I breathe"). And as Sri Aurobindo stressed, aspiration is an intransitive verb. It has no object. As soon as we put "something" after it, as soon as we give it an object, it becomes but a desire. As the Buddha pointed out, it is our desires that cause our lives to be suffering.

I find it best just to refer to it as the heart yearning upward for the More. That life has a Higher Purpose. But never to name the More, never label the Purpose—never to ground the aspiration.

The loss of Aspiration is endemic in all of those whose lives are suffering. It is, I believe, an unfortunate prerequisite for perhaps most, if not all, chronic illnesses. It only reappears when the illness is truly cured, not just the symptoms relieved. In many ways the cure may be seen to be the restoration of Aspiration.

So to help the sufferer regain his Aspiration, or in many instances to gain it for the first time, must be a primary desire on the part of the therapist. However, it cannot be the therapist's Aspiration—for that would be to objectify it.

We cannot make the sufferer surrender his heart to the More, to dedicate his life to a Higher Purpose. For a forced surrender is never from the heart. Nor does it necessarily come about through organized religion—those musicians playing in church were, like Beethoven, non-conformists.

I have found that it can be most easily actuated through Art, the High Creative Arts, and most of all Music. It will come about when the sufferer through his own Creativity at last becomes aware of the Muse, the Perfection within himself. In his desire to so bring Her into the world, he so loses himself, he so surrenders his ego, he so opens his heart, that the object of his desire vanishes as a rising mist in the heat. And out of this surrender there is at last Aspiration.

Then he learns to bring this Aspiration into all of his life, so that it now has a Higher Purpose (which remains unnamed). From this will come his cure. However, if he sets out to play the music, or to live the life, so as to get the Aspiration so as to bring about the cure, then there will be no cure. For that would be merely for a lower purpose, from the mind, and Aspiration is from the heart.

> *O search and see: turn your eyes upward: open, O thou World*
> *Of Love and Harmony in Man. Expand thy ever lovely Gates!*
> —BLAKE

Walt Whitman's *Leaves of Grass* went through six editions, from the first of 1855 with twelve poems to the last of 1892 with 383. There is ongoing debate and discussion as to which is better—for which there are many definitions. This is mine:

The first is distinguished by Aspiration, arising out of Whitman's mystical experience which was the stimulus to his poetry. However, increasingly in later editions the mind supplanted the heart.

> *When I'm painting and I start to think, everything collapses.*
> —CÉZANNE[53]

Perhaps Whitman lost his Aspiration on the Civil War battlefield, or with the near-fatal illness he contracted there, and probably more so later with his stroke. What a tragedy for him—and for us.

Read the "Song of Myself" in the first edition, "one of the great poems of modern times."[54] Feel his Aspiration! Be inspired! Here are the first three lines:

> I CELEBRATE myself,
> And what I assume you shall assume,
> For every atom belonging to me as good belongs to you.

ANOTHER BOEHME?

love is the creator and preserver of life.

—Jacob Boehme,
Mystic and Shoemaker

One of the holiest men I ever knew was a humble shoe repairer who, in the basement of his house, made orthopedic shoes for crippled children. That was all he appeared to be doing, as far as you could tell.

But with everything he made, with everything he said, and every smile he gave, there was something More. Life for him had a Higher Purpose which guided his ministrations to the little sufferers.

He who would see the Divinity, must see him in his children.

—Blake

THE FIVE THERAPEUTIC CRITERIA

BASED ON THE BUDDHA'S four Noble Truths which were previously mentioned, I have found over many years of clinical experience that there are five criteria, which, when met, can best ensure a satisfactory outcome from the therapeutic relationship. These are:

1. The insightful recognition that there is suffering, pain, dis-ease in your life.

2. That you accept responsibility—not blame—for this.

3. That you know that, deep down in yourself, you have the inherent Power to overcome it.

4. That you want me to help you learn how to activate this Power, so as to enhance your Life Energy to achieve Positive Health.

5. That you then want to use your newly found Power to help other sufferers find theirs.

THE THIRD THERAPEUTIC CRITERION

*The natural healing power within each of us
is the greatest power in getting well.*

—HIPPOCRATES

MANY SUFFERERS WHO FULFILL the first two therapeutic criteria have trouble with the third—to have even an inkling, an intimation, that deep within they have the Power to heal themselves.

In most cases this problem is easily overcome with Music.

I just get them to sing opera. Yes, we all can! The technique doesn't matter, only the passion, the Power.

For a man, I tend to use the tenor aria "Nessun Dorma" from Puccini's opera *Turandot* (Puccini is the most passionate), encouraging him to sing out, especially on the final "vincero!" For a woman, again Puccini, usually the first few lines of the soprano aria "O mio babbino caro," from the opera *Gianni Schicchi,* hitting the high note on the word "bello."

They break out into a broad smile, often laughing joyously at their release, at the release of their Power.

Or I encourage them to play a large jazz drum kit: two twenty-eight-inch bass drums, a snare drum, a few toms, half a dozen cymbals, woodblocks, and bells.

Again they laugh! And again they now know that they have the Power—and that It *can* be released.

ALL AS SPIRITUAL BEINGS

HELPING A SUFFERER to make music doesn't, by itself, help him to realize that he is a Spiritual Being, which I believe is the only true "cure." All music making can help him realize that he has a Muse, but not to realize that his Muse is Spirit and therefore not to achieve the ultimate realization that he is a Spiritual Being.

The easiest way for the sufferer to realize that he is a Spiritual Being is for him to be encouraged to find this spirituality, this Spiritual Being, this Muse which is Spirit, within the music, the composer, the instrument, the audience, the therapist, his mother—to reach out beyond himself to find the Spirit.

My belief is that the "ultimate cure" occurs when the sufferer realizes that he is a Spiritual Being. I believe that this can only occur when he first realizes this about another. And every other is his mother, and it is ultimately in her that he must find the Spirituality before he can find it in himself.

In a therapeutic situation, the doctor must first find his patient as a Spiritual Being and then encourage him to see another as a Spiritual Being, the doctor himself. Thus a True Therapy situation would be one in which the doctor sees his patient (equals the doctor's mother) as a Spiritual Being, and the patient sees the doctor (equals his mother) as a Spiritual Being. It can become, as it were, a mutual recognition of the Spirituality of the other, thus of one's own mother, and thus of one's self.

This blessing should occur with a patient at every session, but for the doctor with every session with every patient. This is the supreme gift given him.

It is not enough to help a person realize that he has a Muse. He has to realize that his Muse is Spirit—and This he first finds in another.

There is nothing that is not Spirit.

—MANDOOKYA UPANISHAD

THE LOVE OF MUSIC

The greatest aid to the practice of keeping God
in memory is . . . music.

— VIVEKANANDA

IN MY GROWING-UP years I had many fights with my mother. Immediately after them, I would retreat to my little room and start to brood hateful thoughts that even now, so many years later, I am reluctant to confess. But within only a few minutes I would suddenly feel an overwhelming drive to play a record and almost immediately the hatred would disappear, and my pulse would settle, and my breathing, previously so disturbed, would relax. Then I would want to apologize—sometimes even doing it.

I somehow realized, even then, that my love of music was related to my love of my mother and her love for me. I could so easily feel her love—I just had to play a record.

This has been one of the greatest gifts of my life—whenever I hear Music, I feel loved.

In the darkest days of my first marriage, there was a period when, for the only time in my life, I turned my back on Music. As soon as I realized this, I embraced Her once again, as I did my wife. But she didn't want to listen with me. In the loneliest nights after our eventual separation, music was always there. I felt loved, as if my mother, as Music, was always with me, as she had been in spirit when I was a child deathly ill in the hospital. To listen to the radio was to have her with me, comforting me. I still remember one of the songs that most drew her near, "You're the Only Star in My Blue Heaven."

Except for that one brief period, I have always loved music and, more important, felt loved by it. Not just loving one particular piece of music, or even one genre, but loving all of music, loving Music.

And so I am continually surprised to find that most people, deep down, do not feel the same way. They cannot proclaim with deep sincerity, "I really love Music!" and, even more important, "Music really loves me!" This is understandable with professional musicians who have suffered many traumas, so many heartbreaks associated with music. But it also applies to most other people, including nearly all the so-called music lovers. Whatever they may think they feel, unconsciously it is not the love of music, but rather the rejection of it. With their minds they may embrace it, but not deep down, with their hearts. So they experience so much less of the glory of the Healing Power, of the Love—the Maternal Love, which is Music.

The very reason for being unable to feel this love and give love in return is that they do not feel loved by their mothers. For music comes from the mother, especially her respiratory movements when you are in her womb, then her rocking, her lilt, and her lullaby. Music is mother, music is her movement.

Once they find their mother's love, then and only then can they embrace music, for now they can embrace their mothers. Thus music is the easiest way to feel most loved by your mother. But how to embrace it to feel your mother's love, when it is the not feeling her love that holds you back from the music?

What was it in the music that enabled me to feel my mother's love, in spite of my hatred? Was there some particular way I listened to it, and responded to it, that helped me, and may now help others?

I believe that the answer lies in the way I perceive music: not so much as sound, but as movement.[55] Music first comes to us in the womb as the movement of the mother's respiration: her breath, her *ruah*, her spirit. (Remember that the words *psyche, soul,* and *spirit* come from the Indo-European root *bhes*, "to breathe." And the origin of these words is said to be alliterative, imitative of the sound of breathing—I believe, of the mother's breathing.)

I always feel myself being moved by the music—moved not emotionally but physically. As if I am being breathed, moved, danced by it.

Sometimes I feel this movement in my mind and through my body, without moving externally. But usually my physical body is also involved. Not conducting the music—that is only on the beat, not dancing to it in the more usual ways—for that is too exaggerated. But rather just submitting to the pulse of the music and letting my body be moved by it. I surrender to the pulse of the music, I surrender to the movement of my mother.

Know in your heart that Music is your mother as Love—and surrender to her.

He would gaze into the distance, his features as radiant as those of a youngster in love, his hands and especially his fingers outlining in the air the curve of a score like the physical contours of a lover's body.[56]

—WERNER THÄRICHEN,
on Wilhelm Furtwängler

MUSIC, TRUTH, AND MOTHER

Music is a greater revelation than all wisdom and philosophy.

—BEETHOVEN

MUSIC REVEALS MANY PROBLEMS which would otherwise not be apparent. They are there, but deeply buried. Music brings them out and up to the surface, where they are then manifested, and, of course, where they can now be much more easily overcome. Music reveals the deepest. Its honesty forces these problems to the surface—where they can at last be dealt with through play, Aspirational Play.

How does music do this? When we sing or play it is then that we basically are forced to address our attitudes to our mothers—the source of music. Now all the positive and the negative is revealed. All the aspects of love of mother, and hatred of mother.

You might say that music is like a potion of truth: *In cantu veritas.*

The ultimate therapeutic power of music is that it brings to the surface all the problems with the mother, and it is the problems with her that basically cause all of our problems throughout life. Furthermore, it brings to the surface all our love, and our Belovedness from her. This is our ultimate Healing Power.

Music can be the greatest therapy because it most easily and most completely brings all the problems of mother to the surface—all the troubles in life, and also all of the solutions. For everything is the mother, all problems and all solutions.

THE COURAGE TO HAVE INSIGHT

The unexamined life is not worth living.

—SOCRATES

To SEE OURSELVES as we really are, we must look inside, deep inside. This is the path to Enlightenment, the true and complete appreciation of our Existence.

And this takes courage, for we believe that inside ourselves is "badness," evil, sin. For such is our societal teaching.

The courage to have insight will come when we catch even a glimpse of our inherent "goodness," our Perfection. This we can achieve most easily and readily through Creativity, initially especially with Music.

Then, and only then, will we at last discover our inner Nature, our true Selves.

Knowing that Nature never did betray
the heart that loved her.

—WORDSWORTH

The trust to look inside.
The trust, and faith,
the courage
to look inside.

The courage to have insight, to be deeply honest about ourselves, will come when we get a glimmer of the Perfection, the Muse, which is within us. This illumination most often starts with music, true Music.

INSIGHT AND *INSIGHT*

W<small>HO AM</small> I?

The Divine under many disguises.

—T<small>HE</small> M<small>OTHER</small>

There are two insights: the superficial one: the realization and acknowledgment that our lives are suffering; and the deeper one—the INSIGHT that we are Perfection.

It is the first that prevents us seeing the second. And it is the absence of the knowledge of the second that prevents us seeing the first—and thus seeing the second.

Catch-22?

Not if you catch the Music.

I want to be your healer.
Of what?
Your spiritual suffering.
But first you must admit
you have it.

SINGING THE PULSE

The human being is a singing creature.

— VON HUMBOLDT

YOU HAVE READ, no doubt, many strange things in this book.[57] This may be one of the strangest.

I've said earlier that I've tried to make my writing itself therapeutic—that by your act of reading it your Life Energy may be enhanced.

One of the ways I have sought to achieve this is to make it singable, as best as I can. Not singable like song lyrics, rather more like chantable. Encouraging you to sing along, moving with its flow, its pulse, its pulsations.

I encourage all my students to sing along in this way—not setting the words to music but releasing the music that is in all writing. Nudging the speech into music, like a horse from walking to canter.

We start with Blake, Scott, and Lawson, for they have such strong, easily felt pulses, and then with any poetry, then prose—and even, at the end, the newspaper. The more they feel the pulse, and the more they move with its movements, and then release the movement into song, the more their lives are enhanced.

And I hope it may be so for you with my writing.

RELEASING THE MUSIC WITHIN

I GREW UP LISTENING to a jazz program on the radio every Saturday morning. Even many years later, when I had become more heavily involved with other music, nonetheless, every Saturday morning I found myself usually without any forethought once again listening to jazz. I was going to say playing jazz—but I didn't play it. I only played the records. I never believed that I could.

Now I do! I play jazz on the drums—a complete jazz kit. And I play it every day. A recording engineer once remarked ruefully, "If only the musicians I record loved music as much as I do." Well, my friend, there is a stage beyond that—to play music having spent most of your life believing that you couldn't. Then you really love it, so gratefully.

It is this that I encourage in all the sufferers I meet: play the music within you. You want to, desperately—as desperately as it yearns to be released by you.

I am satisfied . . . I see, dance, laugh, sing.

—WHITMAN

MUSIC—PERFORMANCE OR THERAPY?

The object of all music should be the glory of God.

—BACH

I ASK THE JAZZ MUSICIAN what is his major musical criterion for perform-ance. He replies that he has two. The first to get the harmony, pitch, and meter just right, and the second that the audience like it and pay him.

His purpose in making music goes no higher than this, and he is not the exception: nearly every professional musician that I have known over the years is no more aspirational than this, although some may profess to be.

He would sooner play at the jazz club as an entertainer than in a hos-pital as a healer. He is no different from most musicians, just more honest.

When I play in a pub, I look at the half-glazed eyes of the audience. What do they want me to do? What do they want from me? Just some momentary minor pleasure. I want to help them with their suffering— but I can't get past their glaze.

It is so different in a hospital: the eyes are open, imploring help. My music can go right into their eyes and then deep down to their suffering souls.

SURRENDERING TO THE MUSIC

By sound we go to silence.

—Maitri Sutra

What to do when you have finished playing? Don't just get up and walk away. Sit quietly, silently. This is the most important time. Let the music you have created flow through your body. Feel the Life Energy. Feel it in your hands and feet, in your belly and chest, feel it everywhere. Realize how deeply and easily and rhythmically you are breathing. You may well feel that it is not you that is breathing, but rather that you are being breathed.

Feel the burning flame in your heart that your playing has ignited. Feel it radiating out from you to your loved ones, and further and further.

Feel the peace, know the Love. Not only that you yourself are loving, but that you are being loved: that the music, the world, the mother, loves you. Give gratitude, open-heartedly, for this state of Belovedness.

You find It not by bringing the Music to you but by surrendering to It. You have entered the Land of Music. You have an intimation of Heaven on Earth—a hint of our Perfection.

And through your music, your aspirational play, your action meditation, you have arrived at silent meditation.

A time may well come when the music may not be needed at all. You will not have abandoned it but will have played it at an ever higher vibration, so it becomes inaudible, but ever present, ever enhancing.

THE LAND OF LOVE

LOVE CANNOT BE DESCRIBED; it is beyond description. As Rumi wrote, "Love is a stranger and speaks a strange language." No one tried to write more passionately, more intensely, more devoutly, about love than he.

Let's now consider music. Most people talk of music giving rise to particular emotions in them—sadness, joy, sorrow, whatever. After many years of listening to music, and playing it, and especially working with so many musicians from the most unskilled to international professionals, I have become increasingly convinced that music when properly approached, or rather when we let it approach us, gives rise to no emotions at all.

It is instead as if we become transported by it to another Place, to a Place beyond emotions, where there is no sadness or joy or whatever. Where there is instead . . . what am I to call it? That other world, that other plane of existence, which is Love. The work doesn't matter, or the performance, but rather the desire to be so transported, the desire to go to the Land of Love. It is then and only then that we recognize the truest Beauty and the deepest Truth, the incredible Power of music, of all the creative arts. But we cannot describe what they do because that Land is beyond description. Poets and musicians, as well as the great mystics and spiritual leaders, can at best send back but a postcard.

Over the years I have helped many students to enter this World through music. They always respond by enthusing that now they somehow hear it better, know it better, feel it differently. But they can never describe what the difference is, for again it is beyond words, it is paraverbal.

How to get There? First, suspend all judgment: the music is not good or bad, high energy or low, right notes or wrong, tempo too fast or tempo too slow or tempo just right, acoustics good or acoustics bad, or whatever. Suspend it all, detach yourself from all judgment and just accept the music as it is: as an expression of Godliness, of Perfection, of Love, of Belovedness. Just accept it as Existence. Then we are prepared to enter the Land through Music.

Music is the vehicle, the ferryboat, the guardian angel, that leads us to the Land of Love.[58] I see music as a guide to the Muse, the Perfection within. And it is the best route, for it is the easiest. All we have to do is to suspend judgment and let it take us to its Home.

> The ferryboat
> to the Land of Love
> runs on music.
>
> Hear the singing
> over the waters.

FAITH IN MUSIC

ALTHOUGH IT IS SOMETIMES shaken, my wife and I have great faith in Music. Here are three related variations on this theme.

Some years ago I had two operations under general anesthesia.

The first was in New York. As the anesthetic started to work, the large circular operating light above me became a glistening cymbal vibrating at an ever-higher frequency. Just before slipping away, I thought, "If this is death—it's Wonderful!" To die to Music! Such Music!

I awoke in intensive care, oxygen mask still on, to find myself singing! And singing Irish folk songs—because I had already realized, although not yet fully conscious, that the nurse had an Irish accent.

The second operation was in Vienna. This time I awoke to find myself singing German songs! And I got some of the nurses to sing with me— and even one of the patients.

Then my wife, an opera singer, barely conscious under deep intravenous sedation for a surgical procedure, sang one of the arias sung by The Queen of the Night from *The Magic Flute*! With absolutely no memory of singing it—she only knew of it because the surgeon later thanked her.

If only we all were singing—always.

As an animal species, the human being is a singing creature.

—BRUCE CHATWIN

To die
never having released
the music inside you,
is indeed a tragedy.

THE MOST HEALING TAPE

I'll be loving you, always.

— IRVING BERLIN

I WATCHED A FASCINATING TV documentary in which patients under surgery had hypnosis tapes played to them: positive affirmations by their surgeon, given with all of his authority and dedication. The results seemed most impressive—and even if not, it still should be done, because we all, deep down, know it is right. It feels right.

But, I wondered, could there be a more therapeutically powerful tape? More powerful words—and Music. And given by a loved one, a Beloving one.

What tape would I want to hear? It's obvious—my Beloving wife singing "Always."

I'd like to work with the surgeon to record the patients' spouses singing to them—with the greatest Love.

Remember, it is not the therapeutic power
of your music that heals another.
All your music can do is to actuate the Healing Power
within the sufferer.
It is always His that heals him,
as it is always Yours that heals you.

Your music for another is but a catalyst.
And always remember that every sufferer,
no matter how desolated,
—still has the Healing Power, the Perfection, within him.
Your music acts merely as a reminder.

PAIN BUT NO HURT: MUSIC AND THE MOTHER

THE AUSTRALIAN PSYCHIATRIST Ainslie Meares, dedicated to the alleviation of human suffering, would travel to many far and exotic lands to learn from the healers and wise men of many varied cultures.[59]

His greatest revelation came in Katmandu from a yogi saint 134 years old who meditated for sixteen hours a day. Ainslie Meares asked him if he felt pain. His reply was that of course he did, but—and this was the revelation—*the pain did not hurt.* There is a great difference between pain and hurt. Pain is an essential concomitant of our existence—but it need not hurt. With this new understanding, Ainslie Meares gave up his psychiatric practice and devoted his last years to teaching a system of meditation based on the concept of *pain but no hurt.* This became particularly important in his unique approach to meditation for the overcoming of cancer.[60]

Pain is our response to the shaping forces of our life: to the Tao, the Way, to our karma, to our destiny. Every day we are subjected to these shaping forces by whose means we evolve. These pains are a natural component of our growth: they are growing pains. But they need not, should not, hurt.

As the clay on the Potter's wheel is molded so are we, always with the Potter's intention for us to become more Beautiful, more Perfect, evermore in His image. If the clay were sentient, it would feel pain—but never hurt.

Hurt is an accretion that we add to pain. Pain is perception, hurt apperception. What Ainslie Meares learned and then taught was that there is no reason why there should be hurt. It can be eliminated, and then we can just grow with the pain, grow because of the pain.

Consider the difference between these two statements: "I have a pain in my stomach" compared to "My stomach hurts." Pain is usually used as a noun, but hurt as a verb. And verbs imply action. Hurt is a transitive verb: the pain is in my stomach contrasted with my stomach is hurting me—my stomach is attacking me. This is the psychological component, the hurt, superimposed on the physiological, the pain.

Pain is perceived as internal, but hurt as external. My pain is my doing, my hurt has been caused by another. Pain is in the heart, whereas hurt is peripheral, as if coming from the outside, from another—the mother.

Pain, as I have said, is the workings of the Tao on us: being shaped, being molded, being unfolded, for us to be evermore spiritually evolved.

Hurt, on the other hand, we believe in our unconscious, comes basically from the mother. If only she really loved us there would be no hurt as we move through life. Remember when you were a child and you were injured, you would run to your mother and she would put her arm around you, comfort you, smile on you, and the hurt would go. The pain would still be there, for the nerve endings were inflamed, but there was no hurt. Pain is manageable as long as it doesn't hurt—as long as we believe that we are loved by our mothers.

I believe the ultimate purpose of healing is to help us find the love of our mothers, her divine maternal instinct. It is always there but so frequently it is obscured. And it is the task of the healer to part the sufferer's cloud of unknowing to reveal to him his mother as an earthly manifestation of the Mother of All, the Mother of All Ever Smiling. To know his mother as Her overcomes all hurt and enables him to accept gratefully the growing pains, the workings of the Tao.

Listening with my third ear to my patients' complaints—divorce, disease, whatever—I hear and feel their pain and their hurt. And I've come to realize that there is little I can do, should do, for their pain. But there is much we together can do for their hurt. As they come to feel loved by their mothers, and the world as Her (as it was at their beginning), then there is no hurt—and the pain is accepted, gratefully.

We can accept all of life, all of its vicissitudes, without any hurt, and regard them all as an expression of the Love when we believe that we are beloved by our mothers—and only then. And it is this belief, this knowledge in our hearts of her belovedness, that enables us to respond with love to her, and, then to all as her.

I believe that this is the purpose of music—not entertainment music but true music, what I call metamusic. *Meta* means beyond, and metamusic is beyond the usual music, beyond the mundane. It is music that invokes the spirit. It is music as our mother most loving.

Of all the creative arts, music most has this power to remind us of her belovedness, to help us feel it and live in response to it, free of all hurt. For music comes from the mother: her love is the origin of all music. Her cradling, her rocking, and especially her voice and her lullaby. And always her smile: her smile of comfort, her smile of love.

To hear metamusic, to take it into your heart, is to once again know your mother as the Mother of Love, as an earthly manifestation of the Mother of All. To know your mother's soul.

This is the basic reason for music. In this state of Belovedness there can be no hurt, for hurt is when we do not believe that she loves us. And all is love, when we know that we are being shaped by the guiding hands of the Potter.

It is very enlightening that Ainslie Meares's book starts with his meeting the yogi saint and ends up with his discovery of a Kwan-Yin statuettte that he worshipped as an icon: his Mother of Love.

And thus through it he came, I believe, to find his own mother as Love—and so was free from hurt. Like the yogi, he felt pain, but it did not hurt.

And so it can be for us—when we find our mothers as Love.

> Metamusic transports us
> through our mothers
> to the Mother of All.

BEYOND MUSIC

. . . to penetrate into that region where the air is music.

—EMERSON

HOWEVER MUCH I MAY teach, and preach, of Music, I am always aware that behind It also dwells the waiting Silence—the grateful Silence of Absolute Belovedness.

> There is
> "an understanding beyond words"[61]
> and
> a Land beyond Music.

MUSIC-MAKING AS ACTION MEDITATION

I will sing with the Spirit.
—1 Cor. 14:15

THERE CAN BE NO DOUBT of the infinite importance of meditation. It is not a question of whether one should, but which way may be best for each person.

Most of the forms of meditation with which we are familiar, while inwardly very active, are externally passive—little, if any, movement of the body. One of the underlying principles seems to be that to still the mind, to concentrate it, one must be physically still, inert. You might call this passive meditation.

There is also action meditation, Karma-Yoga. This has been thought by some of the great masters, for example Swami Vivekananda, to be more suited for the Western mind, at least initially. Action is so much more part of our Western culture.

I have found over my years of clinical research that most Western-ers are actually in one most important parameter negatively affected by their practicing passive meditation. The enforced bodily immobility cre-ates in them a deeply unconscious anger, which, although they are unaware of it, affects them quite profoundly. Often they seem to be more like imprisoned captives, outwardly controlled and restrained, but inside seething. Whenever they have instead adopted a more active meditation, especially music, they change, remarkably. Less angry, more loving, and more outwardly directed.

For passive meditation is inward—into the self, egocentric. Whereas action meditation is outward, into another (and every other is, basically, the mother—the first Other).

So it is my belief, arising out of my clinical experience, that for us Westerners, at least initially, action meditation is preferable. Of all the forms of activity, that which most raises the Life Energy, the Love within, is music—especially singing. And of all the instruments, the one that can most so enhance our life through music is the drum, the simplest of all instruments, the oldest. With it, and singing with it, we can greatly enhance our lives and the lives of those for whom we play.

The great Zen master Dogen taught that the purpose of meditation was not just to still the mind *per se,* for that is but a mechanical exercise, nor is it to achieve Perfection, but rather to realize that we are already Perfect. Then, having found It, to lead our lives accordingly.

But this is still a selfish activity. It is preferable by far, and much easier, to first find the Spirituality in another. When we have found it out there, then, and perhaps only then, can we find It inside ourselves. I believe we can only find our Perfection when we have found it in our mothers, our primary Object, the primary One.

I further believe that our task in life, our ultimate aspiration, our supreme meditation, is the joyful, ever-grateful reunion with the Mother who was, and is, our mother: to find the Perfection as it was, and is, in her—that *is* her. This reunion is the highest yoga: union with the Divinity that was our mother's when we were inside her womb and when we were on her belly and her breast. Her smile was the first vision of Love; her body rhythms, her lilt, and her lullaby the first Song of Love.

She was not perfect—the task for the human mother is much too difficult. But she was motivated by her Perfection. Her Intention, her Aspiration, was always of the most loving, but often she failed in practice. Dogen taught that we are all Buddhas, but there are lazy Buddhas, dirty Buddhas, all sorts—and all Perfect.

And to the baby the whole world is his mother, and so it is, in a way, still to us as adults. The audience is the mother, and how you feel about her, how close or how distant you are to recognizing her Perfection, will determine whether or not you are afflicted by stage fright.

The Earth, too, is our mother, and how we feel about her determines whether or not we desecrate it.

Thus music—all of it, the rhythms, the notes, the chords, the motifs, the lyrics—are the mother. So is the composer, and the instrument—all is the mother, and all is Perfection.

Music as an action meditation has as its motivating power the Aspiration to find the Spirituality, the Perfection, the Godliness, which is in our mothers, which is our mothers, which is everyone and everything, and which is us.

Through Music as this aspirational action meditation we can, I believe, most easily find our own inner peace, our Heaven on Earth. Through it we find the Perfection in the song, in the drum, in our mothers—and then in ourselves.

Only then can we feel loved, truly loved, only then are we in the blessed state of Belovedness.

So many meditations, active as well as passive, are cool. Music, True Music, is hot, passionate, for its expression comes not from the brain, but leaps up as flames from the heart.

THE TIDE AND THE PULSE

"THERE IS A TIDE in the affairs of men," Shakespeare proclaimed. Not a force or power, or a direction, but a tide.

A tide: ebb and flow, ebb and flow. Movement, always movement; ever changing yet ever recurring. Always advancing through time—to where? To where? Back and forth, round and round, and on and on.

I stand on a cliff in Sydney overlooking Bondi beach which I have loved all my life, and I realize it is not the sand or the water that draws me, but the waves, the exquisite dancing creations of tide and wind, of Earth's turning, of the dance of sun with moon.

I watch as each of them washes over the rock beneath me, each forming its own pattern of movement, of white, of life. Each forward and back and around and around—and then on to the next, and the next, and the next.

And I start to move with the waves, to dance with them as they flow over the rock covering it, revealing it, and covering it again. Each with its own delightful dance. "When you do dance, I wish you a wave o' the sea." Shakespeare knew. Oh yes, he knew.

Of course God is a singer—every Mother is. But if he also plays an instrument, then he is certainly a percussionist, not a violinist, or, God forbid, a pianist! For it is not the notes he cares about, not the much vaunted harmony, but the basic rhythm, the propelling power, the pulse itself. It is to this that I dance with the waves. "When you do dance, I wish you a wave o' the sea." Shakespeare knew. Oh yes.

I do not know what Tao meant to the ancient Chinese, but certainly its translation into The Way is quite inadequate, colorless, bland, lifeless somehow. There is a sense of direction, yes, but not of movement, of propulsion, of power. All this the word *Pulse* possesses and so much more: the Pulse is love. It is the sound we hear inside the Mother's womb, back and forth, back and forth. And when She cradles us in Her arms and rocks us back and forth, it is to the Pulse, always to the Pulse.

This is the "tide in the affairs of men." And it is this Love that impels the tide as it always has and as it always will: the pulsation back and forth, from her heart to ours, and from ours to Hers: back and forth, around and around.

> The Heart
> of Love
> impels
> the Pulse.

LIFE AS ANANDA

Ananda: Perfect happiness or bliss.[62]

AN EIGHTY-TWO-YEAR-OLD MAN, one of the healthiest I know whatever the age, glowingly informs me that he wakes up every morning glad to be alive.

Not just glad not to be dead, but Glad to be ALIVE!

And he celebrates LIFE through dance and song, but also in all that he does throughout his day. His days, his life, is one of Cantillation, a song of love for the Love.

He tells me that but a few years ago he was in deep depression over the loss of his wife and his work. And it was music that transformed him, not just any music, but Music—Aspirational Play. He has, I believe, found True Joy, *Ananda*.

And he gives us an intimation of It when we sense his Emanation.

every particular Form gives forth or Emanates
Its own peculiar Light, & the form is the Divine Vision
And the Light is his Garment.

—BLAKE

The facts we have
already,
so many
weighing us
down.

Instead,
we need to be
lifted up
on the wings
of Aspiration.

XV.
CONCLUSION

TO THE READER

I LOOK AT YOU, INTO YOU, to see the Perfection that is you—the being you aspire to become — and I try to help you to find This, and to find It in your mother: the Mother she wanted to be.

Then I ask you to do the same with me.

I use words like *love* and *spirit* freely in my writings and this invites judgment. But try to see me not as I am, not as I do—but as I really am: the being I aspire to become.

In the body there are invaluable and unknown treasures.
In all its cells, there is an intensity of life,
of aspiration, of the will to progress
which one does not usually even realize.

—THE MOTHER

TO BE LIKE OSLER

I HEED THE GREAT PHYSICIAN, Sir William Osler, who exhorted the medical students at Yale to "join the whole creation of animate things in a deep heartfelt joy that you are alive, that you see the sun, that you are in this glorious earth which nature has made so beautiful, and which is yours to conquer and to enjoy."[63]

I play music, sing, dance, write, compose, photograph, and draw. All to find the joy, the light, and the beauty.

Sometimes, just sometimes, I succeed. It all depends on my sincerity and dedication—on whether my Aspiration is high.

WORKING FOR THE WORK'S SAKE:
THE *GITA* I

IN MY QUIETER MOMENTS, I think of the teaching of the *Bhagavad Gita:* "these works should be done in the freedom of a pure offering, and without expectation of a reward."[64]

I have the right to work, but for the work's sake only. I have no right to the fruits of the work.

There should be no attachment to the results—for the sufferer, or for me. I must remember that Aspiration has no object.

Just to do the work—gratefully, zealously, passionately, wholeheartedly. To do it because it is there to be done.

THE WORK—THE WAY:
THE *GITA* II

This is the unmistakable teaching of the Gita. He who gives up actions falls. He who gives up only the reward rises. But renunciation of the fruit in no way means indifference to the result. In regard to every action one must know the result that is expected to follow, the means thereto, and the capacity for it. He, who, being thus equipped, is without desire for the result, and is wholly engrossed in the true fulfillment of the task before him, is said to have renounced the fruits of action.

— GANDHI

WE MUST SEE OUR PROBLEMS, our suffering, clearly, truly, honestly. Then go into action to overcome them, for, "He who gives up action falls."

We must have a clear goal before us—a strong therapeutic intention: "one must know the result that is expected to follow." We must become aware of our Healing Power: "the means thereto, and the capacity for it." And be deeply committed: "wholly engrossed."

There must be no "indifference to the result." We must work to be well, for Wellness is the result. We must continually strive for the result. But remembering always that our Work is to do the work. Whatever the outcome, having thus "renounced the fruits of action."

Enjoy the Work, for its own sake. For that is our Way.

REFLECTIONS

REFLECTING ON WHAT I have written, I see four interconnected books, all to do with healing.

It is, first, a self-healing manual for all sufferers.

It is also an attempt to extend the horizon of the treater, encouraging him to become a therapist, as it likewise encourages his patients to become students.

It is as well an instructional book for the holistic therapist to help him further his understanding of his profession, and to increase his healing powers for his students—and for himself.

And, last, it has been a self-healing book for me. Through writing it I have come to a better holistic understanding of myself—as I hope you have come to about yourself.

NOTES

1. Dante, *Vita Nuova*. New York: Oxford University Press, 1992, p. xxi.

2. *American Heritage Dictionary*.

3. See my book *Holism and Beyond: The Essence of Holistic Medicine*. Bloomingdale, Illinois: Enhancement Books, 2001.

4. *Oxford English Dictionary*.

5. See my book *The Healer: Heart and Hearth*. Bloomingdale, Illinois: Creativity Press, 1998.

6. *Volumen Medicinae Paramirum*, trans. Kurt F. Leidecker. Baltimore: Johns Hopkins Press, 1949.

7. *Reveries of the Solitary Walker*, trans. Peter France. Harmondsworth, England: Penguin, 1979.

8. From Jefferson's draft of the *Declaration of Independence*.

9. *The Divine Comedy*, trans. C. H. Sisson. Manchester: Carcarnet, 1980, p. vi.

10. "Observations on Psychotherapy of Schizophrenia" in *Progress in Psychotherapy 1956*, ed. Frieda Fromm-Reichmann and J. L. Moreno. New York: Grune & Stratton, 1956, pp. 245–246.

11. *Mirage of Health*. New York: Harper and Row, 1959, p. 130.

12. Ibid. (both quotes), p. 131.

13. *Strength to Love*. Philadelphia: Fortress Press, 1981.

14. F. C. Happold, *Mysticism*. Harmondsworth and London, England: Penguin, 1990, p. 172.

15. See my book *Life Energy*. New York: Paragon House, 1990.

16. "Observations on Psychotherapy of Schizophrenia" in *Progress in Psychotherapy 1956*, ed. Frieda Fromm-Reichmann and J. L. Moreno. New York: Grune & Stratton, 1956, p. 246.

17. See page 133.

18. See my *Life Energy*.

19. See my *The Re-Mothering Experience.* Valley Cottage, New York: Archaeus Press, 1981.

20. Walter B. Cannon, *Bodily Changes in Pain, Hunger, Fear and Rage.* New York: Harper and Row, 1963.

21. Bruno Bettelheim, *Freud and Man's Soul.* New York: Knopf, 1983, p. 109.

22. See my *Life Energy.*

23. From the Indo-European root *bher*, to carry, from which is also derived *bear, burden. Bher* also meant to bear children, hence *birth* and *fertile.*

24. See my *Life Energy.*

25. George Goodheart, *You'll Be Better: The Story of Applied Kinesiology.* Geneva, Ohio: AK Printing, 1985, Chapter 21, p. 7.

26. Ibid.

27. See my *Life Energy.*

28. From the Latin *ludere*, to play.

29. Artie Shaw, *The Trouble with Cinderella.* New York: Da Capo, 1952.

30. *The Chinese Written Characters as a Medium for Poetry.* San Francisco: City Lights, 1968.

31. Bruno Bettelheim, *Freud and Man's Soul.* New York: Knopf, 1983, p. 35.

32. Another was Louis Cholden, see page 48.

33. *Tolstoy and History.* London: Orion, 1996, p. 1.

34. Freud actually used the word *Trieb.* A better translation than *instinct* is *drive.*

35. Robert Fulford, D.O., *Dr. Fulford's Touch of Life.* New York: Pocket Books, 1996.

36. See my book *The Way of the Pulse: Drumming with Spirit.* Bloomingdale, Illinois: Enhancement Books, 1999.

37. *Of Two Minds: Poets Who Hear Voices.* Hanover, New Hampshire: Wesleyan University Press, 1993, p. 79.

38. F. C. Happold, *Mysticism*.

39. See my *Life Energy* and my *Your Body Doesn't Lie*. New York: Warner, 1980.

40. "He knows peace who has forgotten desire." *Bhagavad Gita*.

41. *The Complete Works of Chuang Tzu*. New York: Columbia University Press, 1968.

42. See my *Life Energy*.

43. *Tao Te Ching*, trans. Stephen Addiss and Stanley Lombardo. Indianapolis: Hackett, 1993.

44. Robert Fulford, D.O., *Dr. Fulford's Touch of Life*.

45. Bruno Bettelheim, *Freud and Man's Soul*, p. 109.

46. Julian Jaynes, *The Origin of Consciousness in the Breakdown of the Bicameral Mind*. Boston: Houghton Mifflin, 1976.

47. *The Chinese Written Characters as a Medium for Poetry*.

48. "Structure determines function." George Goodheart.

49. *The Idea of the Holy*. Oxford: Oxford University Press, 1950.

50. However you choose to define Him, Her, or It.

51. And the use of "it" is also reification.

52. From the same etymological root as "spirit."

53. I am reminded of Chuang Tzu: "Artisan Ch'ui could draw as true as a compass or a T-square because his fingers changed with the things and he didn't let his mind get in the way." *The Complete Works of Chuang Tzu*, trans. Burton Watson. New York: Columbia University Press, 1968.

54. Walt Whitman, *Leaves of Grass*, ed. Malcolm Cowley. New York: Penguin, 1986, p. x.

55. "The content of music is tonally moving forms." Eduard Hanslick.

56. Trans. Henry Pleasants. *Opera Quarterly*. 1995.

57. I initially wrote, "You have, no doubt, read . . .", but changed it to the above because it is more easily singable.

58. Heinrich Zimmer, *Philosophies of India*. Princeton, New Jersey: Princeton University Press, 1969, p. 474.

59. *Strange Places and Simple Truths*. London: Souvenir Press, 1969.

60. *The Wealth Within*. Melbourne: Hill of Content, 1978.

61. Zen master Dogen.

62. *The Essential Aurobindo*, ed. Robert McDermott. Hudson, New York: Lindisfarne Press, 1982, p. 285.

63. *A Way of Life*. New York: Harper and Row, 1937.

64. *Bhagavad Gita*, trans. Juan Mascaro. Harmondsworth, England: Penguin, 1962, p. 105.

JOHN DIAMOND, M.D.

D.P.M., F.R.A.N.Z.C.P., M.R.C. PSYCH., F.I.A.P.M., D.I.B.A.K.

DR. JOHN DIAMOND is a Fellow of the Royal Australian and New Zealand College of Psychiatry, a Foundation Member of the Royal College of Psychiatrists (UK), and is a Fellow and past President of the International Academy of Preventive Medicine (US). He has held numerous senior clinical and university teaching appointments in clinical psychiatry, basic sciences, and the humanities, has lectured extensively throughout the world, and is a best-selling author.

Dr. Diamond is concerned with all aspects of the totality of the sufferer. His forty-five years of research and practice in medicine, psychiatry, complementary medicine, and holistic healing have led him to investigate many modalities which affect body, mind, and spirit.

He has over many years employed Creativity, especially the High Arts, regarding them as an essential and major component of Healing, and has founded The Institute for Music and Health and The Arts-Health Institute to train those interested in learning how to use the arts as a therapeutic modality.

In his teaching, writing, lectures, and private practice he draws on insights from all of his experience to provide guidelines for holistic living. His approach combines the idealistic and the practical, supplying tools each individual can use in all aspects of life, both professional and personal. Dr. Diamond practices as a Holistic Consultant in South Salem, New York.

For more information, please contact:

The Diamond Center
P.O. Box 381
South Salem, NY 10590

Phone: 914-533-2158
mail@diamondcenter.net
www.diamondcenter.net

The Diamond Center
PO Box 381
South Salem N.Y. 10590
Phone 914 533-2158

W W W. Diamond Center. net

DR. George Goodheart
Robert C. Fulford
Robert Livingston
Desmond Swan